Hi, Attention of Joe Duffy show.
I'm a self-published Irish writer o
Dublin but living now in Rossla
life seemed to be getting short l
to self-publish. I'm a member of the Irish writers
Union and have in the past completed courses with the
Irish Writer's Centre and Writer's Digest School in Ohio.
I regard myself as quite prolific & previous works
include The Scribe, War, Raw, Die Bergtruppen, Exile,
Wolf Neumann, The Pitboys (included here), Sorting out
Charlie, Snowrun, Orphans, Mano, Manhunt, Pacific
Deeps and others.
I'm attached to buythebook.ie

The Nationalists

Irish., Volume 1

Liam Robert Mullen

(Irishwriter)
kirkusreviews.com/author/liam-
mullen-edit1

I have a kirkus proconnect page.
I'm also attached to the Green Dragon in the UK.
My Amazon author Page is amazon.com/author/
liammullenauthor
This book was a featured book on Wattpad
in its earlier stages.
Blogs at freelancer555@wordpress.com
Also facebook@ irishwriter112 also goodreads.com/irishwriter112
@liammullen555 (twitter)

Published by Liam Robert Mullen, 2018.

The Nationalists
By
Liam Robert Mullen
Copyright 2016 Liam Robert Mullen
License notes. 2016.

THE NATIONALISTS

First edition. November 20, 2018.

ISBN: 978-151 909 4179

Written by Liam Robert Mullen.

CHAPTER 1

SURRENDER!

The word hung in the air like a weapon, dripping with venom.

The very thought was shocking. Days of fighting reduced to this. Tony McAnthony looked at the broken faces around him. He could see pride and courage, but he could also see defeat. And huge bitter disappointment.

Some fighters lay unmoving. They'd given their lives for their vision of a free Ireland. Shattered glass, and broken chairs and debris lay everywhere. Some had been hammered into rough wooden barricades and shooting vantage points. Papers were scattered

1

along the marble floor; post office documents, stamps, food coupons, ration cards.

Days earlier, McAnthony had watched from the roof of the General Post Office, as several of the Rising leaders had broadcast the Proclamation to the world. Radio was still in its infancy, but the hope was that the broadcast would reach the ears of those who mattered in America.

McAnthony pondered his own fate. Would the British accept that he had been a non-combatant? He'd disobeyed his editor at the Times - Conor Sweeney - a good man, but a man with a limited viewpoint. Sweeney had a tendency to take a pro-British view and his views on rebel groups were prejudiced and naturally jaundiced. Perhaps that stemmed from Sweeney's Protestantism background. Tony wasn't sure.

He knew he was lucky to be alive. The Rising had been particularly strong in Dublin, unlike 1798, which failed when Wexford and parts of the North had rebelled but Dublin hadn't risen. This time things were different. Key buildings had been seized in Dublin: Jacob's Biscuit Factory, Clanwilliam House, which dominated Northumberland Street, Boland's Mill, the South Dublin Union and St Stephen's Green, and Dublin Castle. The GPO itself had been taken at the start of the week.

Wexford had again risen to the challenge and in Enniscorthy the rebels held out longer than their Dublin comrades.

The British had been caught with their pants down. Many of their officers had been at the races out in Fairyhouse, and with many people in a holiday mood for the Easter break, nobody had been expecting a Rising.

It had been the perfect time to strike!

The signs had been in the air for weeks. Military manoeuvre around the Castle. Irishmen and women parading with weapons on open display. The Castle men hadn't tried to disarm them, fearing bloodshed, but plans were afoot for a massive round up. Still they had waited too late. A secret council of the

Irish Republican Brotherhood had planned the Rising with such secrecy that even Eoin MacNeill had been caught unawares. MacNeill was commander of the Volunteers, three thousand of whom were Dubliners including the two hundred strong Citizen Army, and the Volunteers probably numbered thirteen thousand on a countrywide basis.

Roger Casement had been sent on a secret mission to Germany to secure arms for the Rising, but due to a series of mishaps he had been arrested on his return and a Norwegian ship - The Aud - which had been carrying a shipment of arms was sunk.

Learning this MacNeill published a notice on Easter Sunday in the Irish Independent forbidding Volunteer movements, but the movement behind the Rising was unstoppable. Though forced to postpone for a day, the orders for the Rising went ahead for Easter Monday. And though confusion reigned in some parts of the country, MacNeill's notice had lulled the British into thinking there was no rush in rounding up armed Volunteers. The British too couldn't go rushing in where angels feared to tread. They needed to avoid alienating both nationalists and unionists up the north who were volunteering for military duty abroad, and the raging war in Europe. Talk of conscription was high on the political agenda, and a hotly debated topic - both north and south.

McAnthony had linked up with the rebels when they had gathered that bright Monday morning at Liberty Hall. A rumour had reached him at the office, which had sent him scurrying from the office, and on a flat run up the quays towards Liberty Hall. He had spoken to a Cork gent who had queried his motives: "You want to join us - why?"

"I'm a journalist."

"Who with?"

"The Irish Times."

"That unionist rag." There was outright contempt in Collin's tones, and a decision appeared in his hazel eyes. His lips curled. He was about to say no.

Tony could be convincing and persuasive when he wanted to be. He decided to be brutally open. "You're right," he said frankly. "It has a very unionist outlook. But that could change some day. You need the papers on your side. I want to report this. It's my job!"

"It's not going to be a picnic," Collins had warned. He pursed his lips thinking. "Your job could get you kilt." The man had a broad West Cork accent. Clonakiltyism was alive in his tones.

"Plus I'm Irish," McAnthony had countered, with a grin.

Collins liked that grin. He'd warned the man. It was obvious from his demeanour though that the man had guts. Collins could relate to that. He recognised a fellow spirit. It might be no harm either to have a reporter from the Irish Times on your side. He grinned in reply.

"Okay then," he relented. "Fall in with the rest."

The march to the GPO had taken minutes. Men from the Dublin Metropolitan Police had grinned at the sight of the marchers, little suspecting that this wasn't a drill.

The citizens of the city mocked and cat-called them.

Volunteers took the building with ease. Post office workers and citizens were evacuated. Where the rebels met resistance, guns were pointed. Warnings issued. Doors were barricaded. The glass in the windows at the ground level was smashed with rifle butts, and men were dispatched to the roof and other floors. Men were stationed at each window.

Padraig Pearse went outside and read the Proclamation. A serious young man, his profile had increased after the brilliant oration he gave at the grave of O'Donovan Rossa, and his voice was clear and precise as he read the Proclamation. People stopped to listen. His voice was heard not just by those in Sackville Street, but by the world. His words rang out:

"WE DECLARE THE RIGHT OF THE PEOPLE OF IRELAND TO THE OWNER-

SHIP OF IRELAND, AND TO THE UNFET-
TERED CONTROL OF IRISH DESTINIES,
TO BE SOVEREIGN AND INDEFEASI-
BLE...IN EVERY GENERATION THE IRISH
PEOPLE HAVE ASSERTED THEIR RIGHT
TO NATIONAL FREEDOM AND SOVER-
EIGNTY; SIX TIMES DURING THE PAST
THREE HUNDRED YEARS THEY HAVE AS-
SERTED IT IN ARMS."

McAnthony was writing furiously in shorthand.

"THE IRISH REPUBLIC IS ENTITLED
TO, AND HEREBY CLAIMS, THE ALLE-
GIANCE OF EVERY IRISHMAN AND IRISH-
WOMAN. THE REPUBLIC GUARANTEES
RELIGIOUS AND CIVIL LIBERTY, EQUAL
RIGHTS AND EQUAL OPPORTUNITIES TO
ALL ITS CITIZENS, AND DECLARES ITS RE-
SOLVE TO PURSUE THE HAPPINESS AND
PROSPERITY OF THE WHOLE NATION
AND OF ALL ITS PARTS, CHERISHING ALL
THE CHILDREN OF THE NATION EQUAL-

LY, AND OBLIVIOUS OF THE DIFFER-
ENCES CAREFULLY FOSTERED BY AN
ALIEN GOVERNMENT WHICH HAVE DI-
VIDED A MINORITY FROM A MAJORITY
IN THE PAST."

Pearse strolled back into the GPO to rising
cheers from his men, and his head held high. McAnthony followed him impressed. He was a very distinctive leader, with an unusual Australian style hat,
and armed with a 7.65 mm Browning automatic pistol.

These men had just declared their own state. He
recognised the significance of the moment. McAnthony had been educated at Trinity College, and he
had studied Irish history and culture as part of his
degree. He could understand the significance of such
moments. Nobody in Irish history had made such
a declaration. It was momentous. He was suddenly
very grateful to Michael Collins for affording him
the opportunity to be present at such a history-mak-
ing event.

A copy of the Proclamation was pinned to near-by Nelson's Pillar, which towered as a symbol of British dominion over Sackville Street. Behind the pillar lay a couple of dead horses belonging to a detachment of lancers who had been caught up in the melee. Four men had been shot dead.

An unreal air hung to that first night with groups of Dublin citizens hanging round gazing at the tri-colour, and the trams and transport off the roads.

Rumour and counter-rumour swept around: THE WHOLE COUNTRY IS UP. THE GERMANS HAVE LANDED DOWN SOUTH.

But it hadn't taken the British long to recover their poise. Within days they had begun shelling their positions. A boat on the Liffey - The Helga - had begun shelling the city. Trained soldiers fired volleys and machine-gun fire raked the rebel positions. McAnthony knew Collins had been right about the dangers when he himself caught a shrapnel blast on the Wednesday evening.

The two Volunteers he had just turned away from hadn't been as fortunate. Both were killed outright.o

Collins flew across the lobby, checking all three men for vitals. Only McAnthony had emerged relatively unscathed. He was wounded, with shrapnel wounds to his back and shoulders, but he was still alive.

It was then he'd met Angela. She had approached him to dress his wounds. She was wearing a long Volunteer coat over her equally long dress, and the dress had a red cross over the firm looking breasts.

Despite his pain, McAnthony was impressed. The women involved in the struggle for Irish freedom constantly surprised him. They took all manner of risks: treating the injured, running messages between different command posts around the city and often when under fire. They too, along with the menfolk, were a force to be reckoned with.

Most of his injuries were in his shoulder and back. She cut away his shirt and working swiftly managed to stem a lot of the blood. She knew by looking at him that he would require surgery, but for the moment she would dress the wounds as best she could. If she could stop the flow of blood...

Michael Collins approached.

"How's the lad?" he asked.

"He's hurt bad," she replied. "Needs hospital treatment."

He nodded soberly. "I'll speak to Pearse. See if we can organise a temporary truce...wouldn't hold my breath."

"Do what you can," she urged.

She continued dressing his wounds as Collins strode away. "What's your story then?" she asked, as she worked away. "How did you get mixed up in this mess?"

"I'm a journalist," he explained, through gritted teeth.

"Yeah. Whom do you work for?"

"The Irish Times."

"I'm impressed," she said. She looked at him with fresh eyes. She had incredible blue eyes. "Will you write about the Rising?"

"That's why I'm here."

She nodded. Her hands were still busy with bloody bandages.

A shell exploded above them somewhere in the building. "Getting intense now," she said. "We may have to pull back."

"Back?"

She nodded, her hands busy. She finished tying a tourniquet and stood. "I'll check back with you later."

"Thanks, Miss."

She smiled. "Na habhar e." Don't mention it. She had a habit of feeding Irish expressions into her everyday speech.

He watched her slim figure making for the stairs. He knew she was heading to see what damage had been done up above by the latest British shell and he wanted to call out to her. He suddenly felt a protective urge. He hoped nothing would happen to her. He caught a glimpse of himself in a broken shard of glass. The chiseled features below his bowler hat, the rough thirty something looks and the slight scar on his left cheek.

Collins reapproached. "No luck. Pearse is negotiating with the British commander, but they won't allow a temporary truce. Pity we could have got you out."

"What now then?" McAnthony asked.

Collins shrugged. "We may need to withdraw. You'll have to take your chances. Come with us."

"Do you think we have any chance?"

"Not much." Collins was reflective. "But we'll probably live to fight another day."

"Any news of other posts?"

"Dev is still holding out. There's been some heavy fighting up near the canal. And at Jacobs."

"What will happen to the signatories if we're forced to surrender?"

Collins scowled. "Don't know, lad. That's bothering me. Has me worried. The British have cut our lines and have taken control of the city quays. They ran a gunboat up the Liffey. They've too many men. Guns. Perhaps we'd have been better off running a guerrilla campaign. As things stand, we have to try and hold buildings. Utter madness."

"You've still achieved something."

Collins grinned, and winking at the wounded journalist, he strode back to the fighting. He was carrying a Lee Enfield.

Tony felt a lot of pain. Every fresh movement brought a new twist of anguish to his thin lips. His green eyes masked a dull pain. Despite his powerful build, Tony, knew he was as susceptible as the next man to a burst of shrapnel. His shoulders were round and broad and it was easy to see how he had once played College rugby when studying journalism at Trinity. He wondered again should he find a safer line of work? But journalism was in his blood. It was his bread and butter. He loved the cut and thrust of his work. He loved in-depth reporting - heavy investigative reporting. He liked the feeling that he was a powerful watchdog for the public interest, and he loved the feeling, and surge of accomplishment, that followed the breaking of a major news story.

A fresh burst of machine-gun fire from outside again intruded on his thoughts. The fighting was getting more intense, he thought. He wondered would he get out of this alive?

He saw a volunteer raise his rifle to fire at something outside. Seconds later the man toppled, his rifle falling from hapless hands, to be picked up by another volunteer. Tony grimaced as blood sprouted from the stricken man's left temple.

The sight of death and war was never easy.

McAnthony had seen enough bloodshed in his thirty-two years on this world. It wasn't a sight you ever got used to. Hardened perhaps, but never quite at ease with the harsh reality of it.

He felt a sudden thirst and made a hand signal to a nearby volunteer who had been assigned to look after the wounded. The man had been attending James Connolly who had taken a shot through the ankle whilst out on patrol. The man approached with a canteen of water.

Tony smiled his thanks. He took the canteen in his beefy hands and lifted it to his mouth. He supped greedily, relishing the cool trickle down his throat. After a moment, he handed the canteen back.

"How's General Connolly?" he asked the man.

"In pain. But he'll live."

The water had been a Godsend. McAnthony appreciated the foresight of the planners who had ensured an adequate supply of water and food. He realized the orderly had been speaking to him and he glanced at the man again, and nodded.

"Yeah, I'm fine," he said. "In pain, but otherwise I'll live."

The man nodded and wandered off to another patient.

Tony caught the eye of Connolly who winked over.

Connolly was an enigma. He was a hero to many of these men here. Not involved in the early stages of the Rising planning, the secret council of the IRB had been forced to include him out of fear that he might start his own rising first. He had been instrumental and had risen to national prominence during the Great Dublin Lock-out of 1913, when Jim Larkin had brought the Irish Transport and General Worker Union to a standstill and had crippled Dublin City.

Both men had made a lot of enemies during that dispute, and Larkin had since emigrated to the States.

McAnthony knew this latest uproar would endear nobody to Connolly. Dublin City had been crippled again. A pall of smoke hung over all the familiar spots - North Strand, the Canal area near Baggot Street, the College of Surgeons, Stephen's Green and Jacob's biscuit factory. Fires glowed orange, but yet the green, white and orange flag proclaiming the new Republic fluttered from the roof of the GPO, where men still fired down on the British troops in the street.

The British had mobilized fast. They were using artillery and machine-gun fire to cow the rebels. Many men had been wounded, and some had paid the ultimate sacrifice. A room had been set aside as a temporary morgue, and as a health precaution.

Every man and woman in the GPO knew his or her job. Some were simply fighters, others attended the wounded, and some were couriers who had the dangerous task of ferrying messages to other command posts around the city. Some were allocated the task of dead body handling; others distributed food and water.

The citizens of the city had been having a field day since the fighting broke out. Many had gone on an orgy, taking advantage of the situation, and looting shop windows. Many lived in the slums surrounding the city. Connolly himself had picked up his wound when he led a group of rebels from the GPO to try and contain the looting hordes.

McAnthony knew that newspaper distribution would have been badly affected by this rising, with circulations stopped. All of the Dublin dailies had their offices in the city - his own paper The Irish Times, The Independent, The Freeman's Journal. Most city businesses would have been out of action since the fighting started, and Tony surmised they wouldn't be a happy lot. He'd never met a business-man who liked losing money. Capitalist blood ran through their veins.

He smiled as he recognised Angela coming back across the floor. Her face wore a worried frown. She approached him, and bent across his shoulder to ex-amine his dressings.

"How are things upstairs?" he asked her.

"Not good," she muttered darkly. "One killed with that last shell. Two wounded."

"Hm," McAnthony moaned. It was becoming obvious that the fight was turning against the rebels.

The heavy machine-gun fire and artillery fire of the British was exacting a terrible retribution and toll. Even the leaders of the Rising were beginning to look worried, and Tony figured it was now just a matter of time before the order was given to retreat. He didn't know it, but for the last few hours Pearse had ordered one of the women nurses to open negotiation talks with the British commander outside.

He saw weapons been gathered together. Orders were shouted to evacuate the wounded first. Angela and the orderly who he'd spoken to earlier helped Tony to his feet. He saw men lifting the makeshift stretcher that Connolly lay on.

Orders were quietly given. Many spoken in the mother tongue - Irish. An air of desperation clung to the rebels, but their spirits and fighting determination remained resolute. The fittest fighters were to remain at their window posts to mask the initial retreat. If the British suspected the pullback they might launch an all out attack. It was vital they were kept in the dark as much as possible.

Shots were still fired by the plucky defenders.

The retreat took place through blown-out walls and tunnels. A fighting retreat.

It was then that the talk of surrender reared its ugly head. The British had snipers taking pot shots at anything that moved within the GPO. The sound of fighting from the Four Courts still reached their ears. Fire and smoke hung over Dublin like a shroud.

The firing was now intense. The rebels began moving back. A secret passageway had been discovered running under Henry Street, and the remaining fighters were retreating as far as Moore Street. The fruit markets had been quiet for days, with no trading during the fighting.

Tony noticed a man - The O'Rahilly - who had been everywhere during the fighting and who had arrived at the GPO in a motor-car laden with rifles, taking fire. He hadn't been popular when the Rising started, because he had tried to stop it, but once in, he was totally committed. When he took lead, he was helped into cover by another rebel - Pairic O'Toole - who had also distinguished himself.

The talk now was of surrender. The Republic had been declared. The fight, for now, was over. Word had been brought to Pearse that the British were ready to accept their surrender. He'd met with their commander - Lowe.

After some brief deliberation the order was given to lay down arms.

They marched out, heads held high. Guns were laid aside. British troops kept them covered with bayoneted rifles, before marching them towards the Rotunda Hospital. Next morning after a bitterly cold night in the open they were marched to Richmond barracks.

The British had always controlled Dublin with a series of army barracks around the peripheral of the city. They blocked off access to the city by country dwellers.

At the barracks 'G' men from the Castle moved among the prisoners, singling out certain prisoners for special treatment. All of the signatories were singled out. Dozens of men and women were pulled aside - anyone perceived by the British and the Dublin Metropolitan detectives as having a hand in the organization of the Rising. Or a command position.

McAnthony watched as Collins approached a young officer, and signalled his head at him. He heard Collin's words: "He isn't one of us. He had no hand in the fighting.""What was he doing there then, matey," the officer barked.

"His job. He's a journalist with the The Irish Times."

The officer looked over at McAnthony with a suspicious glare. Tony made no movement, though his eyes were busy. He had lost track of Angela after the surrender. He wondered had she managed an escape? She was definitely not to be seen.

The officer was reluctant to accept the word of Collins.

"Stand back," he eventually ordered, shoving the young Cork man in the chest. "What's his name again? I'll speak to somebody about him."

"Tony McAnthony," Collins said, unfazed by the push. He watched as the young officer went to speak with a Castle man.

The Castle man glanced over, his keen gaze focussing in on Michael Collins and Tony McAnthony. He approached slowly.

"This man is a journalist?" he queried.

Collins nodded.

"Tony McAnthony?" Addressing the wounded man.

Tony nodded painfully.

"You were caught with rebels...how do you explain that?"

"He snuck in," Collins interjected, lying through his teeth. "Bloody journalists. They nose in on everything."

The 'G' man looked thoughtful. He turned to the young officer. "See that he gets medical treatment, and put a guard on him until we can check him out further."

"Sir," the officer acknowledged, turning to a group of nearby troops and lashing orders for them to carry the wounded reporter to the Castle hospital. He also ordered them to maintain a guard over the wounded man.

McAnthony caught the wink Collins threw at him, before passing out as the four troops manhandled his stretcher none too gently.

The 'G' man hadn't moved. He stared hard at Collins.

"And you? What's your name?"

"Michael Collins."

The 'G' man turned again to the young officer, and spoke from the corner of his mouth. "Special treatment."

"Special treatment," Collins mocked.

"Move you Fenian bollix," the officer said, shoving him towards a separate line where those who had been singled out stood. The 'G' men were beginning to disappear. Collins heard his name being called by somebody, and casually walked over to the other line. Nobody challenged him.

When he looked back nobody had seemed to notice his move. He caught the eye of Dev, who smiled slightly, and motioned him to stay where he was.

Within moments new orders were given and the men were marched off in separate directions.

Martial law had been declared on the city. Special trials were to be held.

CHAPTER 2

MAJOR FRANK CHURCH scowled as he saw his adjutant running towards him at the Curragh racing track.

Couldn't he enjoy a single day off?

The Easter sunshine had put him in a jovial humour, and his luck with the gee-gees had combined to put a rare smile on his face. He knew he was stressed. For weeks he had been monitoring the situation in relation to the Citizen Army and the Volunteers, and he had repeatedly warned Chief Secretary Birrell's office that plans were afoot by rebellious elements for mischief.

"What kind of mischief?" he had been asked.

Church could only shrug. He wasn't psychic. If he knew the answer to that, he'd be able to act with decisiveness.

A product of Sandhurst, Church was not a man who suffered fools gladly. A ramrod, tall man, he had a distinct military bearing and he was intelligent enough to recognise the inherent dangers lurking in Irish politics. He realised that Britain's problems with the Great War represented a golden opportunity for Irish radicals to stage an upset.

His warnings to the Castle went unheeded. Only one man had taken his warnings seriously - Harry Sword - an Intelligence agent working out of the Castle.

It was pointed out to him that Eoin MacNeill had issued orders for Volunteers to stand down from taking any overt action. He was also put in the frame, and was informed on the QT that round-ups were imminent anyway. The capture of Roger Casement had aroused the suspicions of even those bureaucrats who operated out of the Castle, but the belief was that the Rising was months away. An Irishman attempting to smuggle a large supply of arms and munitions from Germany was bound to cause a lot of eyebrows to be raised.

Church wasn't convinced. His sandy coloured eyes betrayed his impatience, and his thin lips curled in contempt as he witnessed what he saw as the ineptitude and inaction displayed by his superiors. Ultimately though he was subject to orders, and he had been ordered not to take any action.

His worst fears were realised when his adjutant reached him and announced, out-of-breath: "M...Major Church," the man said saluting, "Dublin's been taken. The rebels!"

"There's been a Rising?" Church's eyebrows rose as he saluted the man back. "How serious is it, man?"

"V...very serious, sir. They've taken over key parts of the city...folk have been killed."

"Very well, soldier. Round up as many officers and men as you can," he ordered, glancing at his watch. It was half past four. "Meet with me in the corporate tent. I'm going to commandeer that. There will be a briefing at one seven hundred hours."

"Five o'clock. Yes, sir."

"A SERIOUS SITUATION has arisen in Dublin, gentlemen," Church announced.

"Is it a Rising, sir?" a soldier asked quietly. His Irish accent was pronounced.

"Yes...it would appear so, old chap," Church confirmed. "I want all of you men to return to your barracks...muster as many bodies as you can...and remain on heightened alert. I want accurate intelligence reports on the extent of this problem...how many men are involved? In what districts? Is it country-wide? You know the kind of thing. Any questions?"

There were none.

Church wound up the conference. "I suggest, in that case, that we get moving, gentlemen. All progress reports to be channelled through my office. Dismissed."

CHURCH HAD ORGANISED a number of night patrols.

The reports kept flooding in. "Key buildings seized...large bodies of men...the GPO, Stephen's Green, Jacobs. Half-a-dozen other areas around the city. Troops fired on near Amiens St train station...near the Shelbourne Hotel...at the South Dublin Union...near the Four Courts. Fighting out in Ashbourne. Trouble in Enniscorthy in County Wexford.

He amalgamated the reports, sticking pins onto a large map of the city, hanging on his wall. He had heard that General Maxwell fresh from defending the Suez Canal against the Turks had been posted to Ireland to put down the Rising. Maxwell would want a clear understanding of the situation when he arrived.

He ordered troops to set up barricades and man checkpoints. He sensed it was important to cut off links between the various rebel outposts and curtail movement between them.

A giant plan of action was forming in his mind about how to retake the city. It wouldn't be easy. The rebels seemed a determined lot.

Blood would be shed...buildings damaged.

Orders were dispatched. Troops mobilized.

The British had finally woken up.

DECLAN HANNAFIN HELD his hands high as he emerged from the College of Surgeons with the men and women of Michael Mallin's command. The men had been ordered to ground their weapons.

Throughout the week they had held on well.

They had taken St Stephen's Green at the start of the week, but had been forced into a fighting retreat when British troops managed to occupy the Shelbourne Hotel, and were able to raze the park with machinegun fire from the windows of the hotel, and particularly its roof, which overlooked most of the park. The Volunteers had been forced to retreat back into the park, away from the deadly guns in the Shelbourne.

Hannafin was no older than fourteen, but he was an active member of the Fianna - a militant boy's organization that had helped during the Rising. The Fianna was a boy scouting movement, and proved a useful recruiting ground for the Irish Republican Brotherhood and the Volunteers. His blue eyes still shone with defiance, but Pearse had ordered all commands to lay down their arms. He caught the wink thrown at him by Margaret Skinnider - a Scot who had been summoned by the Countess Markievicz, Mallin's second-in-command, back to Dublin to take part in the Rising, and who had distinguished herself in the fighting - and he grinned back.

"Wipe that grin off your face, boy," a British officer warned, "or I'll wipe it off for you."

Skinnider moved closer. "Leave the wee lad alone, and pick on somebody your own size," she hissed at the officer.

He met her steely eyes and backed off.

She nudged him. "Tiocfaidh an lá," she whispered, encouragingly. In Irish. "Our day will come." She eyed the youngster from the corner of her eye - the dark handsome looks, lank black hair combed back, grim expression around the mouth - and concealed a grin of admiration. With youngsters like this rising up through the ranks, Tom Clarke's vision of a rising in every generation would bear fruit. Such thoughts sweetened the bitter pill of surrender.

Markievicz was being disarmed. As the second in command, and President of the Cumann she too cut a dashing figure. She was wearing her green puttees, riding breeches, tunic, a slouch hat with ostrich feather and a Sam Browne's ammunition belt. She kissed her revolver before handing it over - a final act of defiance - that would go down in Republican folklore. She was a legend in Dublin; her estranged marriage had made her a countess.

The prisoners were lined up in two rows. Mallin and Markievicz marched at the head of the column, the soldiers surrounding them on all sides with fixed bayonets. The bayonets were partly for their protection because the crowds watching their arrest were very aggressive. Shouts went up: "BAYONET THEM."

They were marched initially to the courtyard at the Castle, passing a huge pit, which caused more than a few heads to turn. Mallin exchanged a tight look of concern with the countess. She remained unflappable. Stay cool, her eyes suggested. Then they were forced along Ship Street towards Richmond Barracks in Inchicore. Crowds lined the roads waving their hats and brandishing their Union Jacks.

No love was lost between the citizens of Dublin and the captured rebels, but these feelings would soon change.

DECLAN'S TWIN BROTHER Ciaran had also been involved in the fight. He had the same dark handsome features, lank black hair, and the same tough swagger. He found himself under Ceannt's command at the South Dublin Union. The 4th Battalion, Ceannt's command faced heavy action!

They had mustered at Emerald Square on Easter Monday morning and they had taken the huge complex buildings that formed the South Dublin Union - the poorhouse in James's Street - which housed the city's homeless and destitute. The buildings were spread out over 50 acres of ground, with dormitories for over 3000 patients, houses for officials and nurses, churches and hospitals, sheds and workshops.

Ceannt's command was spread dangerously thin on the ground, only sixty men having mustered, when it came time to take and hold this complex, but the command was an important one because of its location. Located as it was on the western edge of the city it controlled movement from the nearby Richmond Barrack's, and its proximity to Kingsbridge railway station, with its terminus of lines running as far south as Cork. Another garrison lay close by - the Royal Barracks, and to the north the Royal Hospital at Kilmainham, and the residence of the British Commander-in-Chief.

Many of the patients couldn't believe what was happening in their midst, and were shunted to buildings bearing Red Cross flags. Ceannt had ordered Hannafin to raise the Irish tri-colour over the west wing of the building complex, something the youngster obliged with, and he was gratified later that it commanded so much attention from a British machine-gunner perched on the roof of the Royal Hospital.

The men under Ceannt's command were a hardy bunch and were in action from the first day. Con Colbert who had once led the Fianna movement as Chief Scout was there, and so was Cathal Brugha who would suffer heavily in the fighting to come. A party of 200 soldiers of the Royal Irish Rifles were sent scurrying for cover when the Volunteers opened on them from point blank range. With so few men at his disposal Ceannt and his men were forced to fight from one building to the next.

Hannafin found he was cut off during one such retreat. A soldier made towards him, and Ciaran fired a warning shot at the man. He turned and raced for cover.

Another man rose from cover nearby and Hannafin recognised Ceannt. The two of them turned into a blind alleyway and stopped confused. There was no way out.

"This is it, boy," Ceannt ground out. They prepared a last stand.

The soldiers had broken off their pursuit. A cautious face appeared in a doorway, and a nun wearing a black and white hood beckoned to them urgently. Ceannt, a Galway hound, needed no second invitation. The two men rushed through the doorway and made it to the apparent safety of a Catholic hospital.

Ceannt grinned at Hannafin and clapped him on the back: "Good man, you're doing a great job."

The main complex of the hospital now became a battleground, and a dangerous one at that. Two British soldiers killed a nurse as she went about her rounds. An inmate was also shot dead during a search, and another was killed in a grenade explosion, and his companions lay groaning in agony after a British soldier flung a grenade into the packed room.

The hospital was a maze of intersecting corridors, with an incredible amount of hiding places, which both sides took advantage of. The fighting continued day after day, from room to room. Close quarter battle, with men's nerves on edge from the bitter close-in fighting. By Thursday the British had built up considerable reserves and were joined in the battle by men from the Sherwood Foresters, and new men drawn from the Curragh. Troops from Athlone and Belfast also came into the fray, and some members of the RIC aided them.

Throughout the week the rebels had held three key outposts, which were instrumental in helping hold off new British attacks. Watkin's Brewery in Ardee Street had been taken, as had Jameson's Distillery in Marrowbone Lane and Roe's Distillery in Mount Brown. Heavy fighting erupted with hundreds of British troops fanning out from the Rialto side, but fanatical rebels who poured everything they had into the British masses held them back. It was during this latter attack that Brugha was heavily wounded, and his deputy William Cosgrave assumed command.

Later that evening the British were again driven back.

Friday brought more skirmishes. A party of British soldiers opened up on their own men that evening bringing a little respite and humour to the rebels. Saturday came and went, and rumours of how matters were developing elsewhere reached the defender's ears. The news was not very reassuring. On Sunday MacDonagh arrived from Jacob's to brief

Ceannt on Pearse's general surrender at the GPO. The order to ground weapons was given.

Ciaran didn't experience the hate-filled venom and abuse that had been hurled at other commands as they were led away under watchful bayonets. Instead he experienced a near euphoria among the population who had gathered to watch, and a rousing cheer greeted his ears as they were led away.

BILLY HANNAFIN WAS a hard, stocky man and the typical average Dubliner. He had married young - a childhood sweetheart. Joyce had made him a perfect wife, and had bore him ten children.

A deeply religious, pious, simple man, Billy could be seen at 11 o'clock mass every Sunday in the Pro-Cathedral. He enjoyed the Latin mass, where the boys of the Palestrina choir sang, and two of his younger sons. It was also the day that Billy and his wife applied a strict dress code to their family. Shirts were ironed, trousers and dresses neatly pressed, shoes buffed to a mirror shine.

Billy was also deeply involved in the community. Having ten children of his own had given him a deep love for kids, and he regularly organised outings, boxing and football clubs for his gang - as he affectionately called them.

Though he would never dream of taking up a gun himself, Billy had a grudging respect for the rebels who had taken over his native city during the Rising of 1916. He had yet to find out that two of his own sons had taken up the fight, but when word was brought to him during that first week that two of his lads were in the thick of the fighting he had been immensely proud. That hadn't stopped him worrying of course, fretting about their safety, but he was proud of the way they'd made up their own minds to become involved. He didn't see it as a betrayal that neither had told him, but he knew from their complicit silence that they were changing from mere boys into men.

The Rising had affected his income for a time, something he hadn't been keen about, with ten children to feed. But by the end of the week he had returned to work, and was once again plying his trade as a labourer on building sites around the city.

Work was slow for a time. Billy was surprised that no immediate attempt was made to clean up the capital street, which months after the Rising still had a dilapidated, warlike look about it. A general malaise had set in, and the economy was bad. The scale of destruction in the capital had surprised him, with brick rubble everywhere. The round dome of the bread factory, diagonally opposite the GPO was also gone, a familiar landmark ground to dust.

Billy liked to read the newspaper once a week, and this kept him informed of wider world events like the war in Europe. Like many Irishmen he feared conscription, and he didn't want to see any of his sons fighting for the Queen's shilling - the flip side of the coin being though that work was scarce and the army could offer regular income. Many working class families had sons in the army.

Perhaps that was why he had felt pride his sons were involved in the Rising. Then again perhaps it was just simple relief that both boys had emerged unscathed.

ENDA MCFRY FELT DISAPPOINTMENT as he moved forward with the rebels from the GPO, with his hands held high skywards.

He was a strategist who had been involved in some of the initial planning stages for the Rising. The overall strategy had been to seize key buildings in the Dublin area, and this planning had seemed to work. There had been some obvious failings in the execution of the planning which McFry would identify at a later date - a key issue with the taking of the Green being the failure of Mallin's command to occupy the Shelbourne Hotel with its fresh supplies of food and water, sheets and blankets, and of course the obvious vantage point of its roof which the British had taken full advantage of to raze the Green with machinegun fire.

He was a studious individual, known throughout Dublin society for his radical poetry, which had been published in socialist newspapers. He was lean, thin and bearded. His views were respected within IRB circles, and he had the kind of magnetic persona that men like Padraig Pearse could associate with. His wife, Susan, was an Irish history lecturer in Trinity College, and like her husband espoused a radical, rebellious attitude to Irish affairs. It was a marriage that worked not least because they could feed off each other's ideas.

Like Tony McAnthony, Enda McFry had identified with the importance of the proclamation when he heard Pearse read it.

The man had a huge respect for Pearse, and he knew that the funeral oration given by Padraig at the graveside of O'Donovan Rossa had changed the perspective of men like Clarke towards Pearse.

A watershed in Irish politics..

Enda caught his wife's eye as he emerged into Sackville Street under the threat of British bayonets, and he gave her an encouraging smile. His wife was dressed in the uniform of Connolly's Citizen army. She was slightly younger than her husband, in her late twenties, with premature greying hair, and she had recently battled her way through a more difficult fight with cancer. Now she had taken on an even greater challenge when she opposed the Crown forces in what was to prove a pivotal fight for the sake of Irish freedom. Her fight for complete freedom manifested itself in the way she led evening classes for children in Irish language and history, and she was a committed member of Inghinidhe na hÉireann - the women's separatist movement who through the use of the classes had pledged to fight for complete freedom from Britain. She was also involved in the Suffragette movement and she was pleased that the new constitution as espoused by

Pearse at the beginning of the week enshrined the rights of women.

She nodded back at her husband, giving him a tight concerned look. Her dusky green eyes couldn't conceal her anguish at their surrender. Her slight shoulders moved in a shrug towards Enda, the question apparent in her posture: What now?

His shrug in reply was one of nonchalance : Let's wait and see. They were marched off in columns, under the basilisk stare of uniformed soldiers, rifles and bayonets at the ready. Alert for treachery.

CHAPTER 3

FATHER JOHN TROY HAD enjoyed the Easter ceremonies.

He always had a special affinity for those special times of the year. Christmas was followed weeks later by a period of self-sacrifice - Lent - culminating in the Easter celebrations of the Lord's passion and resurrection.

The weather this Easter Monday had been as glorious as the Resurrection celebrations the day before, and he had celebrated both days with a Latin mass accompanied by the Palestrina Choir whose music never failed to inspire him. An all boy choir, the Palestrina choir, had been in operation now a good few years and was a spectacular success with the local parishioners. He had donned his black cloak on Good Friday to say the Stations of the Cross, and on Thursday he had been busy with confessions.

What soured his mood on Monday was the startling burst of gunfire near the pro-cathedral.

What was going on?

A parishioner coming from the direction of Sackville Street filled him in. Suddenly everything clicked together in Troy's mind.

He had wondered why confessions were up on previous years, and why men whom he hadn't seen in ages, were suddenly confessing the burden of their sins to their God.

They had been expecting trouble. They were geared up for death. They were wiping the slate clean.

It suddenly all made sense to Troy.

It was a time of change.

Father John Troy moved among the slumped bodies of men who'd given everything for a free Ireland. He had battled with his conscience before strolling the short distance from the Pro-cathedral to the shell shattered remnants of the GPO to give the fallen of the Rising a final absolution. He made no distinction between Irish or English dead. Though his church didn't espouse violence, having decided under Pope Pius to adopt a conservative attitude to such matters as Nationalistic politics.

In Europe a bitter trench war was engulfing nations. Slaughter on a large scale had taken place in Gallipoli only a year before. John Troy knew he lived in troublesome times. He felt it was a challenge to his priestly ministry. He liked working on the edge.

He'd come to the priesthood late in life. What some might call a late vocation, but he'd no regrets about the type of life he'd chosen to live. He'd entered the seminary at the age of thirty-six, three years after he'd made a life changing pilgrimage to the Holy Land. The sense of peace on his return had been remarkable. The sword of the Holy Spirit had pierced his very soul like a long, razor-thin silent shaft of light.

He never knew why he'd never got married. In his earlier years he had yearned for the love of a good woman, and he had gone to the usual dances and social outings, but it just hadn't happened. He'd had the usual crushes on young women, but somehow that perfect happiness had always eluded him. In days gone by it had made him melancholy. Sometimes helpless and sometimes sad. But life went on, and the dark, melancholy days had been swept away like a sting-ray on an ocean current. The tide of that current had lifted him onto a new plateau, and he was no longer drowning like a piece of flotsam, but was instead elevated in a new direction.

There was a smell of death in the GPO, as he moved around congealed blood pools. John Troy was a man used to death. Both his parents were dead, and his only other close family was a married sister who had immigrated to the States. She had three children, whom he'd only met once, having gone on a retreat to the United States. Despite this separation they remained special in his heart.

Troy felt pity as he moved among the dead. The newspapers might be calling this lunacy "Criminal Madness", but these men were mostly young and just days before had been full of ideals for their version of a free Ireland. Troy knew that this particular battle had been going on for centuries. Probably since The Battle of the Boyne in 1690, and he knew also that particularly in 1798, priests - men of his own calling, of his own cloth - had led the rebels in rebellion against Crown forces. It was enough to give any Irish priest with Nationalistic ideals pause for thought.

With his duties done, he emerged back into the sunlight of Sackville Street, and spotted one of his own parishioners approach him. He suppressed a groan when he noticed it was Minnie. Her voice was sharp, accusatory, as she greeted him.

"Father," she acknowledged. "I'm surprised to see you here?"

"Why is that, Minnie?" Troy's coal-black eyes flashed with sudden irritation.

"Don't tell me you're been giving absolution to those monsters."

This was one of the things, which annoyed Troy about Christianity. How some people saw everything in black and white - with no in-between - just a muddy-grey misunderstanding fog of self-importance. A belief that their way was the only way. A misguided arrow of conceit. How they seemed to leave their Christianity at the door of the church as they emerged from Sunday mass. That lack of feeling, of basic human compassion, amongst the so-called pious, offended him deeply, but his voice was still polite, although slightly sharp when he said to Minnie: "And why shouldn't they receive final absolution, Minnie? Aren't they all God's children?"

"They're bowsies," she said, in a shocked, disapproving tone. "Absolute bowsies."

Troy was silent, thinking. Minnie was one of those women who looked like she carried the weight of Dublin on her broad shoulders. Unkind folk in Dublin would have called her an old bat. A battleaxe, perhaps! She was still in her forties, but her face had probably seen better days, and she had the bearing of a much older woman. She was a product of the Dublin slums, having being raised here, and in turn having raised her own family. Troy understood her troubles. With a husband and eldest son off fighting for the British in France somewhere, probably the Somme, she was worried that the money from the Front might dry up for the Irishmen who'd volunteered, and whose cause had been damaged by what she referred to as the 'bowsies'.

Troy could understand those fears. His own background could not have been more different. Growing up in the south Dublin suburb of Booterstown, he had enjoyed a somewhat more sheltered upbringing. His childhood had been cultured - a world of music, literature and poetry. His family were well respected in the community, and his father held an important government post. He had the opportunity to travel from early in his life, mostly to European cities; Rome, Paris, Venice, Berlin, Florence and Madrid. By the time he was a young man not only had he experienced the culture these cities offered, but also he had seen many of the famous art exhibitions these cities were famous for.

Although his working life brought him into contact with the poor of Dublin, whom he could empathise with but with whom he no other real alliance, Troy knew he was at a disadvantage in dealing with these people. But wasn't that the nature of his calling? He moved in different circles - both socially and culturally. He attended theatre regularly, often going to plays at the Abbey where he could culturally converse with the likes of W.B. Yeats and Synge. These movements brought him into direct contact with men and women who could be termed revolutionary, and who used every means at their disposal to push the Irish cause.

Playwrights wrote Irish stories that appealed to the new sense of nationalism that swept the country at regular intervals; sporting heroes played Gaelic football and hurling and intermingled with the same set; and yet others pushed for Irish language teaching to help protect the sense of nationality. Teachers and professors mostly, but the Irish push wasn't confined to academia circles.

The cultural revolution was everywhere.

In literature there was the Tain and stories about mighty Irish warriors like Cuchulainn and Oisin. In theatre houses and on stages up and down the country, Irish plays were shown. Gaelic games were heavily promoted in the sport arenas. Even in mass on Sunday mornings, prayers were uttered in Irish. There were advocates for the use of the Irish language up and down the country. Poems and stories were written in the native tongue. Military commands in the Irish Volunteers were issued in Irish. It was far from the dead language that many folk tried to maintain.

It was 'beo', alive in every sense of the word.

There was a section of society across all social spheres that tried to downplay and undermine this sense of Irish identity, but nothing could stop the forward beat of a nation. Although small in geographical terms, the country was still capable of throwing a mighty punch. A knockout blow!

The Irish identity was ingrained in the national consciousness. It was as real as an ancient stone. Like a stone it was a solid, rocklike feeling as unshakable as faith.

When he replied to Minnie, his reply was cautious. He knew the woman wasn't above writing into the archbishop. "Even bowsies deserve respect, Minnie."

"Ha," she snorted, stamping her foot angrily on the ground. "They should shoot the lot of them."

Troy started.

It was something he hadn't given a lot of thought to. He knew, of course, everyone in Dublin knew, the British had taken a lot of prisoners, but he hadn't given a lot of thought to what might happen to them. He realized he'd been amiss. He should have checked into that. He certainly hoped Minnie's analysis of the situation was wrong, and that no harm would come to the men and women taken captive. He didn't want to see any of them shot, but he realized in his heart that the British might want to make an example of these men. Instead of arguing further with Minnie, he glanced at his timepiece, and told her curtly he had to go.

His steps were energetic as he left the GPO and hurried towards a tram that would take him to the Castle. Suddenly he felt an air of hurry and of urgency, almost panic. He wasn't a big man in size, but in stature his parishioners all looked up to him.

He ignored the nods of deference directed in his attention when Dublin folk noticed his collar. He sat alone, staring gloomily out of the window. His reflection stared back at him - the furrowed forehead, wide face, thoughtful eyes. His dark hair had greyed, as had his beard. His mouth was tight and grim, his eyebrows bushy above the eyes, his nose slightly askew - broken in a 'rugger' match when he was younger. He wondered how he could have missed the signs? Confessions had been unusually busy all weekend. Easter confessions always brought out the sinners, but this year had been particularly busy. A lot of tough, fighting men waiting in the pews, kneeling and genuflecting in front of the Virgin Mary, the figure of Christ, the statues of Saint Martin and Jude. Men who wanted to wipe the slate clean - men in the know, who had been forewarned that a Rising was afoot.

The destruction to the city was widespread. He saw the damage the British gunship 'The Helga' had inflicted on Liberty Hall. Luckily nobody had been killed there. Buildings elsewhere were heavily damaged; with smoke entrails and fire damage still visible hours after the last surrender.

He had heard there had been heavy fighting in parts of the city besides the GPO. There was a lot of talk about Jacobs and Stephen's Green and the canal areas.

Minutes later he disembarked at the gates of the castle. There seemed to be a lot of activity. Troy glanced at a stretcher bearing party that passed him as they made for a waiting ambulance. He glanced at the supine figure of the man being borne and started in surprise.

Wasn't that the renowned Dublin journalist - Tony McAnthony who worked for Conor Sweeney at the Irish Times? How had he become embroiled in this mess? Troy knew Sweeney and had shared a cognac with him only two nights ago. The editor had been worried about his ace reporter, unaware of his whereabouts.

He quickened his pace, but was stopped by an armed sentry at the gate. The soldier was brisk, agitated.

"What do you want here, Father?"

Troy was equally brusque. "I want to see the commanding officer."

"Sergeant," the soldier bellowed, deciding this warranted higher attention.

The sergeant was stern in manner. "This is no place for you, Father."

"Who's in command here, Sergeant? I need to speak with him about those men you're holding."

"There's nothing you can do for them, Father. Word is they're bringing in some English officer to look after them."

"Who?"

The Sergeant shrugged nonchalantly. "Don't know," he admitted. He stayed silent a moment, thinking. "Follow me," he decided. "You can speak with our officer commanding."

Troy was led to a general in charge.

"General Blackader," the man said, introducing himself. "How can we assist you?"

"General," Troy acknowledged. He could see the Castle men moving among the prisoners, picking out the likely ringleaders. He nodded his head at the men. "What's going to happen to them?"

The General shrugged. "They're criminals. Murderers. Insurgents. They'll be tried and dealt with."

"Dealt with?"

The General looked uncomfortable. "Yes," he confirmed.

"Executed?"

"Didn't say that, my man. But that decision is out of my hands. London will decide."

"Will they get a fair trial?"

"They'll be tried by a military tribunal," he admonished shrugging.

The General was dismissive and Troy knew the situation had escalated to a point where neither man had the power to change matters. He thanked the man for his time and turned to go. The General had a last word for him.

"Pray for them, Father. It's the best you can do."

Troy nodded sadly. "Prayer is sometimes the last resort of the desperate," he said, softly. "But I will take your advice."

As he turned to go and was being escorted across the stone courtyard, Troy caught a wink thrown at him by a man held captive. He smiled in remembrance. Michael Collins. He'd met that young Cork lad at a recent function in the city - perhaps the Abbey. Lady Lavery had introduced them.

He decided to walk home. Walking sometimes allowed him to think well, and he wanted to see the effects the Rising had had on his native city. He took a roundabout route, heading towards the Grafton Street area of the city, and around by Boland's Mills where de Valera had commanded. The damage was evident everywhere. Townsfolk huddled in tight knit groups, talking quietly among themselves.

There was a subdued mood, palpable even amongst visitors. It hung to the very air. It drowned out the holiday atmosphere, which had been very much in evidence only a week before. It drowned out the familiar Dublin undertones and intonations. It threatened to submerge the feelings of the populace as surely as if the black waters of the Liffey had risen and exploded upon the city in a giant tidal wave of emotion, and an outpouring of grief for their stricken city, and not a little bit of nationalistic triumph and pride. Dublin had risen; Ireland had awoken.

Troy was very subdued as he reached home. He decided to pen a letter to his archbishop to see what could be done for the imprisoned rebels.

He sat heavily on a Victorian armchair as he took up his writing pad and pen. Archbishop Raymond Tuite was a powerful figure in the diocese, but Troy didn't hold out much hope for the man's intervention.

Tuite wouldn't want to antagonise Rome.

Rome!

Long the seat of power to St Peter's successors. Though an eccliastical headquarters in the Vatican, Rome had always had its finger on the pulse of politics, and its watchful eye on world affairs. A particularly keen eye was kept on Ireland - the country being a strong bastion of Roman Catholic values.

Rome recognised the loyalty value of Catholic Ireland and was well aware of the numbers it provided in building up the church and sending its men and women on the foreign missions.

It had observed the outbreak of a rising with misgivings, but also with a strange understanding. It understood the needs of small nations to throw off the shackles of oppression. Wasn't that what the war in Europe was all about? Tiny Belgium was the classic case of a country, a Catholic one at that, that bigger nations were fighting desperately over.

The Vatican wasn't happy about the blood being shed in Europe, but its ambassadors were powerless in the face of the European armies and their leaders. It could only sit back and watch, offering advice from afar, from its seat in Rome.

When the letters from the Irish bishops arrived in the Eternal City, the Vatican pondered on what moves it should adopt. In many ways they adopted a wait and see attitude, but they also exerted a quiet influence.

The politicos in London felt that pressure.

CHAPTER 4

MAJOR HARRY SWORD WATCHED as James Connolly was stretchered out of his cellblock and propped in a chair to face the firing squad. May had arrived with a vengeance, but the promise of summer held no hope for those who had been condemned to die.

The man met his end bravely. Sword sighed.

He had tried to stop these executions. His reports back to London had warned of a hardening attitude among the Irish people as each new execution was announced. Sword had been an intelligence officer for a long time, and he recognised the danger signs when he saw them. He could sense the shift in mood whenever he walked around the city of Dublin.

Most Irish people had thought the executions would end with the first three - Pearse, Clarke and MacDonagh.

Sword himself hadn't thought that likely. Sword was a razor-thin man, and he walked with a slight limp. A year before he had been posted on the Turkish beaches in Gallipoli, and he had been shot in the foot. He hadn't been sorry when his recall papers came through - Gallipoli had been a mess. He still had nightmares about it. His features were almost cadaverous, but his dark eyes had a hint of sympathy and intelligence in them. He had watched the demeanour of men like Pearse both as they stood in the dock and in front of the firing squad. The Irish rebels had impressed him.

Following on from their deaths though a further four were shot by firing squad - Willie Pearse, a brother of Padraig, Ned Daly, a brother-in-law of Tom Clarke, Michael O'Hanrahan and Joseph Plunkett. The following day Major John MacBride defiantly went to his death. His estranged wife, Maud Gonne, was living in Paris with their son at the time. Sword got word from fellow intelligence agents that she had immediately donned black clothing on hearing of her husband's fate.

His death was followed by Sean Heuston, Michael Mallin, Con Colbert and Eamonn Ceannt. Mallin had taken control of St Stephen's Green during the Rising, and his second in command had been Countess Markievicz, whose death sentence had been commuted. In Cork, Thomas Kent, faced a firing squad, at Cork Detention Barracks. The last two executions took place back at Kilmainham when Sean MacDermott and James Connolly were shot.

Bitter antagonism also surfaced across the nation when men with nothing to do with the Rising were arrested and shipped off to internment in England.

The drawn out nature of the executions had a significant impact on the mood of the Irish people, who if the truth were revealed, began having sympathies with the rebels from the very first night they were held under bayonets at the Rotunda Hospital. The Rotunda's surrounding black spiky railings had prevented escape. Rumours had circulated of abuse and torture. It had been a bitterly cold night.

Sword had heard those rumours, and his enquiries revealed that a British officer had acted in a brutal manner towards the prisoners. Sword couldn't do much about it, but include it in his reports back to London. He didn't know it then, but that British officer's actions had made him a marked man, and the officer would pay for his folly in Wexford in a few years at the hands of some of those imprisoned.

As an intelligence officer, Sword thought his superiors had made mistakes in their selections of who had to die. He couldn't see why Willie Pearse had been put to death, even though he was a brother of Padraig. Other execution choices had also given him nightmares. One man whom Sword recognised as highly dangerous stood out by a good country mile.

The rebel's men referred to him as the Chief, and Sword recognised the awe the rebels held him in - Eamon de Valera.

Sword had investigated the man's background. He knew the man had commanded the 3rd Dublin Battalion, and that he had been appointed to his position by Pearse in March 1915, that he had taken control of Boland's bakery mills in Grand Canal Street. Morale had certainly been very high throughout his command during the Rising, something that indicated to Sword the calibre of the man leading them. He had also been concerned with Thomas Ashe who had made his presence felt in north county Dublin, and knew that both Ashe and de Valera had been the last to surrender.

However when Sword tried to make his points known, he was told in no uncertain tones to mind his own business, and his views were thrust aside. He was told to get back to his job - which was intelligence. He was left with the distinct impression that it was a failure of intelligence that had led to the Rising.

Sword didn't even try and answer that one. The Rising wasn't his fault. He wasn't taking the blame for that one. No way!

THE EXECUTIONS SHOCKED Troy.

He had done what he could by intervening with the British authorities, but to no avail. He realised that in the wake of the Rising his own attitudes had changed. He still abhorred the use of violence especially for political gain, but he was intelligent enough to recognise why certain individuals recognised the power of the gun. He felt himself that the key to real change lay in the power of the ballot box, and he would be surprised if the Home Rule party still called the shots after the next elections.

The British were compounding their problems, thinking wrongly they would teach the recalcitrant

Irish a harsh lesson, but in reality they were creating martyrs for the cause.

Would they never learn? Troy sighed heavily.

HER MOTHER HAD DIED when she was six, so Angela O'Sullivan assumed her politics arose from growing up in an all male environment. Her father had always had staunch Republican views, and he had instilled his own set of values into Angela's brothers in particular. She had five older brothers, four of whom were married today.

Her eldest brother had remained a bachelor, working a farm in County Kerry, which her father had retired from due to ill health. Two of her brothers had immigrated to the United States like many Irish folk before them. Another was about to be imprisoned by the British in the wake of the 1916 Rising - he'd been with Dev in Bolands. Another was in a British jail, convicted on bombing charges. His wife lived in England.

It was little surprise that Angela had become mired in the politics espoused by both her father and brothers, and indeed many of their friends and neighbours. As a child she'd become something of a tomboy and could hold her own in any argument amongst the men. She'd grown into a beautiful young woman - but she still carried that rebellious nature that had been ingrained in her every fibre since her childhood.

At twenty-five she had joined Cumann na mBán, though she'd been involved in nationalist movements since her teen years. An all-woman organization this band of dedicated women put forward the kind of ideas and ideals that a young woman like Angela could relate to. When she'd heard details of the Rising, Angela had felt excitement and had no hesitation in volunteering for the assault on the GPO. For weeks she'd been involved in manoeuvre with the men of the IRB.

Cultural nationalism and militarism had merged in the few years since Angela had first joined the Cumann. Since Larkin's lockout in 1913, new forces were emerging and amalgamating their strengths, forging together in new alliances, a great meeting of minds and hearts. They were united in one cause - a free Ireland. Home Rule was high on the political agenda, both in Westminster and back home in Ireland. In fact so focused were the British on Home Rule issues, that even their media missed the vital signs in Sarajevo that triggered World War One. But England's misfortune was Ireland's opportunity, and although John Redmond of the Home Rule party pledged Irish volunteers for the British war machine, others saw the opportunities that this war might bring them.

Arthur Griffith's paper Sinn Fein had lambasted the policy of Redmond of the Home Rule Party, and James Connolly was equally vitriolic in the Workers' Republic.

An astute young woman, Angela O'Sullivan recognised the opportunities that this conflict brought for Ireland and she was able to empathise with leaders like Griffith and Connolly. They were men of vision. She recognised that. She knew that their dream was her dream. The dream of every true Irishman and woman. It was no empty eggshell. The desire for nationalism wasn't Ireland's alone. Egypt and India also hungered for their independence, and were also subject to British Imperialism. Hungary had obtained a measure of independence, and her case was being closely examined by the likes of Griffith who could see parallels with the Irish situation.

Canada too had won dominion status from Great Britain. Iceland from Denmark.

It was easy to see where the real concern of the British lay. They were worried about the breakup of their Empire. A lot of their powerbase was taken up with the Empire...to lose that power on the world stage was unthinkable.

The O'Sullivans were a proud Kerry family, beholden to no man or woman, least of all, a foreign Crown. They owned their own land, and had sweated and toiled the land for more years than they cared to remember. They had survived the Famine years back in the 1840's. They were proud to live in a Republican stronghold.

It was in such an atmosphere that Angela and her brothers had grown up.

Angela had managed to escape the round up at the end of the Rising. A friendly Moore Street trader who knew her family managed to hide her. It was one of the few houses in Moore Street that wasn't in smouldering ruins. Martial law had been declared in the city, making it dangerous to move around. But through her contacts, Angela learned the fate of the captured rebels. She heard they had been rounded up, and marched off to various locations. That evening she teamed up with some more women she knew and they went up to one of the hospitals. Many of the dead had been taken there. Bodies were piled high, and it was the first inkling they had that the killings throughout the Rising had been widespread. A number of civilians had been killed.

Word had reached them of rebellions in other parts of Ireland. The north had been a maelstrom of confusion due to McNeill's countermanding order of Easter Sunday. Confusion had reigned in other parts of the country too, though a large force of men in Mayo, under the command of Liam Mellows, had risen.

As she moved through the makeshift morgues, Angela was moved to tears. Was it worth paying these kinds of prices? she wondered, in the all out attempt to win control of an Irish Republic. So many had died. Young and old!

She wondered what had happened to McAnthony. She hoped the journalist had remained unscathed by the scythe of death, which had swept through the men, women and children of this room. She wondered too on the fate of her brother who had been fighting with Dev's contingent in Boland's Mill - the youngest member of the clan Tadhg O'Sullivan.

Talk was mixed on the streets. Some favoured the rebellion, most disapproved.

The most disapproval came from those with loved ones in France, who had hopped on the recruitment tram in Dublin city, bound for a stint in the British army and the fighting waging in France. Those who were receiving the Queen's shilling had the most to fear. Would their money be cut off, in protest?

Angela made her way back towards Moore Street. She would stay there for a few nights before moving on. As night fell the streets fell quiet, and it became dangerous to move around. Curfews had been declared. The British patrols were edgy. They would shoot first and ask questions later. Cordons were everywhere. Soldiers checking papers, searching for weapons.

Her friend had been busy over the stove she noticed as she entered her home. She joined them at the kitchen table and was handed a steaming bowl of Dublin coddle - the famous Dublin dish that included pork sausages, bacon and kidneys, potatoes and onions all boiled together. She had first met Lucy Corish at a ceilí when the young Wexford woman had arrived in Dublin looking for work, and before she had met with Ben.

She ate reluctantly, sparingly. She toyed with her spoon. Her appetite wasn't the best since the hospital. Her friend's kids were also quiet, which was never a good sign in itself. Kids were usually noisy. She allowed herself a quick glance at the man of the house and saw him watching her with a baleful glance. He was a giant of a man, but with a gentle disposition. His moustache bristled with unbridled indignation. He obviously didn't approve of the rebels, but like many an Irishman he knew enough to keep his 'trap' shut in front of his wife. He towered over his wife, but Lucy called the shots in this home. He was also the silent type, preferring to eat his evening meal in brooding silence. Her friend, Lucy, sensing the strain kept up a light-hearted banter throughout the meal.

Angela gave her a hand with the dishes afterwards. "Your husband, Ben, doesn't seem too happy."

"Ach," she replied. "Ignore him. He's moody because he can't go out for a pint." Lucy Corish was a waspish, stunning blonde, with pale Irish features, marked by a generous mouth and smile. Her dark eyes danced merrily. Her wiry body had been attacked with each new birth, and though she still had a good figure, the four children she had conceived were beginning to tell on her body.

"It's more than that, I think," said Angela, flicking a strand of her dark hair away from her eyes.

Lucy polished a bowl with a teacloth before replying. She was studious about hygiene, her home always spotless. "You know Ben. He's a staunch Catholic. He doesn't approve of all this killing. Thinks the rebels are a rabble bunch."

"They are not rabble, Lucy."

"Agreed," she replied. "But Ben has strong views."

"I'll move on in the morning," Angela decided.

"Where will you go, luv?"

Angela shrugged. "Might go home for awhile."

"To Kerry?"

"Aye."

Lucy finished off her dishes. "Well...you take care girl. It's still dangerous to move around."

"I'll be okay," Angela said.

Lucy slapped the finishing touches to her kitchen. "Why not join us in the parlour for the Rosary," she said. Saying the Rosary was one of those old Irish traditions handed down through generations.

Angela thought of the hundreds, perhaps thousands, killed in the last week, and gave a weak grin. "Why not?" she added simply.

"IS SHE GONE? BEN CORISH asked.

"If you mean Angela," Lucy replied, "yeah, she's gone. No thanks to you, hon', she continued in her broad Wexford accent. "You could have been more polite, more welcoming."

Ben's face flushed.

"Polite," he growled. "Go out and take a look at the streets, Lucy. That's what she and her friends did. She's good riddance."

"She's my friend," Lucy said quietly. "And what's more...you have a short memory, Ben. Have you forgotten how she helped us when we moved back from England?"

Ben was silent. "I don't want her around here again, Lucy."

Lucy's temper was beginning to boil. "That's tough," she said, "because she'll always be welcome in my home. If you can't stomach that, then make yourself scarce when she's around."

"This is my home too," he growled.

"She helped us get this place. Or have you forgotten that already?

"I haven't forgotten anything, but I don't want her around. She's a bad influence on the kids. Did you see Brian going to school this morning? He has

one of those republican badges stuck to his school-
bag."

"You made him take it off, didn't you?"

"I don't want my kids growing up like that, with
rebellion thoughts like that outfit who wrecked the
GPO last week. What were they trying to achieve
anyway? Answer me that?"

"An Irish Republic, perhaps?" she suggested angrily.

"An Irish me arse," he retorted angrily. "They've
no more chance of winning an Irish Republic than
the Germans have of winning in Europe. Look
around you, woman. Have you seen the streets...the
rubble...the damage in the streets. It will take years to
repair. Years."

She said nothing. There was no talking with him
when he was in this type of mood. Ben lapsed into a
moody silence.

BEN CORISH WAS HITTING the bottle.

Since Lucy had taken in Angela, he had maintained a snooty silence with his wife that persisted days after Angela had returned to Kerry.

Lucy had ignored his moods. What she couldn't ignore though was his drinking.

Night after night he was coming in half-baked. She had nearly reached the end of her tether.

She knew she'd have to tackle this problem head on. There could be no ducking the matter.

On the Friday night when her friend Angela was singing her head off in a Kerry haybarn she decided enough was enough. "Okay," she burst out belligerently. "Out with it, Ben. What's the matter with you lately? Why are you coming home drunk every night?"

"It's y...you," he slurred.

"What about me?"

"T...taking in that slag from Kerry," his voice rising.

"Ben, she's not a slag. She's my friend."

"She's a rebellious slut," he shouted.

"Ben, there are children in the house," she warned.

"P...pity you didn't think of that when y...you endangered their lives."

She was aghast. "What?" she said.

"Y...you heard me."

"Ben, I'd never place the children's lives in danger. Their lives were in danger all that week. Remember?"

"You shouldn't have taken her in."

She was silent. She had to admit he had a point. But what else could she have done? Angela was an old friend who had needed her help. She said as much to her husband.

He had clammed up.

"Ben, there's more at stake here than my help to a friend. Why are you drinking so much?"

He burst into tears.

She was horrified. She had never seen him crying before. "Ben. What's wrong?"

"They've laid us off," he announced. "Y...your rebel friends have destroyed this city. Buildings smashed to pieces. No work."

So that was it. And he was only telling her now. She felt a surge of anger. "When," she demanded. "When were you laid off?"

"Last week."

"And you're out drinking every night of the week? You should have told me before now."

"I...I'm tellin' you now," he slurred.

That was all she needed, her man out of work. No wonder he was so bitter against the Rising.

She would help him rise above this. She saw it as her duty as a loving wife. Early in her life she had made an investment in this solid man, and she wasn't about to let anything like drink or job loss, undermine that investment or the love they experienced.

Silently she folded her kitchen apron away and she turned to him.

MAY HAD RECEDED AND June had arrived as Angela returned to her home in Fenit. Friday nights in the O'Sullivan home were always a lively affair. The community would gather around. A ceilí or an old fashioned sing-song would commence in the big haybarn and kegs of Guinness would be opened. It wasn't unknown for a bottle of poteen to be passed around. A right old hooley.

She had arrived back in Kerry and had settled in on the family farm. The farm consisted of one hundred acres of rolling grassland, with the upper reaches given over to mountainous terrain, which was used for the sheep. On the lower plains cattle roamed. Some fields were used for tillage - growing potatoes and carrots and cabbages. The farmhouse itself was typical of Ireland - a white washed long barn like structure with a thatched rooftop, small Swiss windows with the glass divided by wooden lattes, and brightly painted doorways, which matched the bright red barn off to the side.

Even in remote Kerry news of the leader's fates in Dublin reached their ears. It saddened her that men like Pearse had been shot. Was that what the British called justice?

Trials were still taking place.

Details had emerged since the surrender. The capture of Casement...the north had failed to mobilise properly...a killing in Cork of a policeman.

There was talk that many of the men had been forcibly marched to ships and herded aboard like cattle. Nobody was quite sure if they were bound for England or France, but within days came news that they had been imprisoned in various prisons throughout England and Wales. Internment camps. Wooden huts surrounded by barbed wire fences and armed sentries.

Angela's heart was hardened though when she heard how General Connolly had been lifted from his stretcher, put into a chair and carried outside to be shot against the cold grey walls of Kilmainham.

Angela who had always had a big singing voice sang several Irish melodies.

She had always maintained an aloof air with any of the local men, but they were nonetheless mesmerised by the haunting sound of her voice.

They sat around the kitchen hearth talking.

Tea was over, and the work of the farm was over for the day. The dishes had been cleaned and put away. Neighbours crowded around the blazing fire, eager to hear the news of Dublin.

Angela's father, Jonjo O'Sullivan settled down in his favourite wicker chair and stoked the tobacco in his pipe. It had always been like this for the Irish, sitting around in front of a fire, telling each other stories. Down through the centuries, folk had lived in clusters known as 'clachans', and within each 'clachan' a tradition of storytelling, music and dance had sprung up. Some of the men sipped surreptitiously - poteen.

Poteen was an illegal brew that some swore tasted better than the legally distilled whiskeys.

Jonjo O'Sullivan had the gnarled, weathered look of an outdoor man, and his blue Atlantic eyes flicked to where his daughter sat, a shawl spread over her knees. Her mother used to sit in that wicker chair. She constantly reminded him of his dead wife - the long flowing raven hair, high cheekbones, curl of the mouth when she was amused, her startling blue eyes which matched the colour of the Killarney Lakes on a sunlit day, her persona, and the confident way she carried herself around. She was a woman who was content with her own beauty, and aware of her effect on men.

"So Angela, tell us about the fight," he said. His ruddy features lit up in anticipation, and he put a match to the tobacco in his pipe. The rich smell of Virginia filled the room. Jonjo liked his pipe.

She told them about how the rebels had taken key positions throughout the city and had held out against all the odds. She told them about men like Padraig Pearse, Colbert, Cathal Brugha, Michael

Mallin. Since the Rising, Angela had managed to piece together what had happened in other posts.

She told them of the fight near Guinness's where Cathal Brugha had been shot twenty five times whilst operating with Con Colbert. Colbert had paid the ultimate price against the walls of Kilmainham. But most of all she told them about the GPO fight where she herself had been stationed during Easter Week.

Her listeners were agog.

One man whistled. "Damn, I wish I could have been there. They put up one hell of a fight."

Angela looked at the man, seeing the look of chagrin in his eyes, knowing he was a member of the IRB. She smiled, her smile mirrored by her brother, Henry, in the corner. Dingle McGee was an old family friend, and the look of chagrin on his slightly disorientated face was totally genuine. The Irish Republican Brotherhood had begun life in 1858, and nine years later would take part in a futile rising, which failed. The seeds of rebellion had manifested itself

further in support of the Home Rule movement organised by Charles Stewart Parnell and Michael
Davitt's Land League. Following a Fenian bombing
campaign in England, after the fall of Parnell in
1891 and the collapse of the second Home Rule Bill
in 1893, new blood emerged within the IRB movement. On the Supreme Council of the IRB was the
one man who had a living link with both risings -
Tom Clarke. Two organizations swung into action -
the Gaelic League and the Gaelic Athletic Association - and Clarke scoured their ranks for new IRB
recruits.

In Ulster Bulmer Hobson reorganised the IRB
with help from Denis McCullough, who came from
a known republican family. Hobson then moved to
Dublin and worked closely with Clarke and Sean
MacDermott to build up the IRB on a national basis, though later Hobson's ideal were to clash with
the other two men.

"And then they were shot?" The IRB man's face
held a pained look.

"In Kilmainham," Angela confirmed.

"How about the people?" Jonjo put in quietly, tapping his pipe.

"They were against the rebellion at first, but when the executions started, something changed. They grew more resentful. Took to taunting soldiers, singing rebel songs, wearing republican badges, hanging portraits in their windows of the slain leaders."

"Pearse started something," Henry O'Sullivan added, his face more composed than the rest. Henry, though rebel blood ran through his veins, was the pacifist among the family, and the one most likely to have sympathy for the victims in this on both sides of the conflict. He now ran the family farm. He was a solid wall of a man, with calm pale blue eyes, and a crooked nose. In his younger days he had boxed and his frame showed that he still possessed that litheness that a lot of sports people possessed. Most folk, especially family and friends called him by his nickname 'Boxer', as a sign of respect and remembrance of the fighting man he had once been.

"Aye, son, that he did," agreed Jonjo. He lifted a glass and proposed a toast. "To our fallen heroes. And a free Ireland."

"To a free Ireland," they chorused.

The clan toasted and began singing. Ballads.

"The Bold Fenian Men!"

TONY WAS SLOWLY COMING out of his antiseptic trance.

He'd dreamt of that young woman who'd helped him in the GPO fighting. He recognised that he had been impressed by her rebellious streak and haughty face with the high cheekbones. He wondered what had become of her?

Her coolness with the madness around her had made an impression on him, wounded though he was. He remembered her dark raven hair, her Kerry accent, and the smooth lilt to her voice that stirred his blood. She had been damned attractive, he thought.

Slowly he was becoming aware of his surrounds, of white-frocked nurses flitting about like nightingales working feverishly. With purpose.

"Sleeping beauty has awoke?" a female voice enquired.

McAnthony's green eyes focused on the speaker, a red-haired smiling nurse.

He smiled, and then grimaced as his movement hurt him. "Where am I?" he asked.

"Hospital, young man." The nurse was in her mid-forties, so in her eyes McAnthony was a young man. He wasn't that young. He'd celebrated his thirty-second birthday last January.

"The Castle Hospital," she explained further, sensing his confusion.

"Terrific," Tony thought. He hated hospitals, especially when he was the patient. Lately he'd spent a lot of time in hospitals, normally as a result of wounds picked up in various conflicts around the globe. He asked a further question.

"You've been here two days, Tony," she said. "You were operated on last night."

"How did that go?"

"No complications," she assured him, "but Doctor Curtain will fill you in later. Would you like some tea, Tony?" She pronounced it 'tay'.

He nodded.

"I'll get you that in a minute, Tony. I'm Helen, by the way."

"I know. I saw your nametag. Nurse Helen."

"Observant too," she laughed. "Not just a pretty face."

"Journalists are paid to be," he told her. He wondered if she was flirting with him or was just making him jolly because of her profession. He decided the latter.

Journalists could also make good judgements.

She was gone for a while but he saw she was as good as her word when she returned with a steaming cup of hot tea and a tray full of cheese sandwiches. Tony was ravenous and said nothing as he wolfed the meal.

She watched in silence as he ate, busying herself updating his chart, which hung at the foot of his bed. "Is there anyone you need to tell Tony about your stay here? Family, friends?"

He shook his head.

She was persistent. "Your wife? Parents? Brothers? Sisters?"

"I'm not married. Parents are dead." He smiled sadly. "Bit of a lone wolf, really?"

She nodded. "Well, we've let your paper know. Your boss - Sweeney, I think he said his name was - was very concerned. Asked a lot of questions?"

"Was he here?"

"Last night," she explained. "Said he'd see you later. Told us to take good care of you. Said you were one of his best reporters. He seems to think very highly of you."

Tony nodded seriously. "Nice to be appreciated," he said.

"You should get more sleep," she advised him.

He closed his eyes as she disappeared down the ward.

SWEENEY WAS NOTHING if not ebullient.

He arrived in the ward the next morning, with newspapers tucked under his arms and his hands full of grapes. He joked good-naturedly with the nurses, even giving nurse Helen a bear-hug which made her blush a deep crimson and wagged his stubby finger at McAnthony as he approached his bed.

"Got a bone to pick with you, lad," he boomed. "What the hell were you doing in the GPO?" Sweeney was a heavily built man, with a jovial round face, and intelligent dark, seadog eyes. Tattoos crisscrossed his thick arms - pirates - in his younger days Sweeney had circumnavigated the globe with the British merchant navy. Twice!

Tony suppressed a groan. He had been dreading this moment. But Conor looked in good mood. Maybe he'd be okay.

"My job," he said simply.

Conor was curious. "What was it like?"

"Pretty horrible," Tony admitted. "But it was glorious too, you know. Something historic. They were very heroic."

"Brought you some grapes. Newspapers," Sweeney said, and hesitated before adding: "They're on trial for their lives."

"The signatories?"

Sweeney nodded. "They've charged close to two hundred, and have rounded up several thousand."

Tony remained silent. Thinking. He eventually looked askance at his editor. "A favour, Conor?"

"Name it, boy," Sweeney said.

"There was a girl involved in the fight. I think she was a nurse - a member of the Cumann. Use your contacts. See if you can find what happened to her?"

Sweeney smiled. "I'll do what I can, Tony."

The two men chatted for a few minutes before, before Tony began feeling sleepy. Conor rose and left the ward.

NURSE HELEN HAD BEEN replaced by the time McAnthony next awoke. A severe looking matron informed him that Doctor Curtain would shortly drop by for a chat about his condition.

Curtain was an eccentric looking individual, his eyes hidden behind half-moon glasses, his white hair unkempt. His voice sounded like a deep bass singer, as he sat casually beside the journalist and boomed: "No serious damage. Nothing that won't mend. You're a young man...you'll recover."

"When can I get out of here, doc?" McAnthony asked.

"What's your hurry, young man?"

Tony grinned. "No hurry. I was just wondering."

"You'll be out by Christmas," Curtain promised, and then seeing the look of chagrin on his patient's face, he relented, and said: "Don't worry. I'm just kidding. We're holding you for a few days observation...just to give your wounds time to heal. You may be left with some scars."

Curtain indicated the spots on Tony's shoulder where it had been necessary to operate and eyed his patient with frank curiosity. He paused, before adding: "Understand you're a journalist? That you were in the GPO during the Rising...what was it like?"

Tony filled him on the details. He finished by saying: "They were very heroic, doc."

Curtain remained silent, thoughtful. Eventually when he spoke his words held a lot of wisdom. "A blood sacrifice always makes a difference with the Irish people. Mark my words. They'll be remembered when all this is long over."

"Do you think a republic will ever be achieved, doc?"

"I've no doubt about it whatsoever," Curtain stated emphatically. "Pearse and them got the ball rolling. A few years down the road, perhaps when this war in Europe is over, we'll have an Irish Republic."

"My thoughts too, doc," Tony said yawning.

Doc Curtain glanced at his watch. "I'd better get on with my rounds. You should catch some sleep, Tony."

Tony nodded as the doc left the ward. Within seconds he was asleep.

CHAPTER 5

DISCHARGED FROM THE hospital, McAnthony noticed the surveillance almost immediately. He was paid to recognise such things.

Castle men, he thought. British intelligence was obviously still suspicious of his motives for being in the GPO. There was nothing he could do about their paranoia. As a journalist though he liked his freedom, and it irked him when he realised that the Castle were tailing him.

He'd heard of the executions before his discharge. He'd read the news of the deaths in the newspapers. He'd heard the fate of Pearse, Clarke and

Diarmiad in the hospital corridors. Spoken of in hushed tones. Snatches of conversation overheard.

"...lined up against Kilmainham wall and shot..."

"...one in that ward. They say he's a journalist. But what was he doing there?"

Mostly condemnatory remarks, but here and there, the odd bit of national pride and rebellious talk. "...bloody heroes, every manjack of them..."

"Lining them up like pigs to the slaughter. Bloody English."

The news had hardened his heart. Once again he wondered what had become of Angela? Had she been taken prisoner? Was she awaiting a similar fate in Kilmainham jail?

He had his contacts. He was determined to find out. He limped towards the tramline in Dorset Street. He'd make for the office.

He brooded on the tram. What was wrong with life when his only visitor had turned out to be his editor - Conor Sweeney? His mood was dark as he climbed slowly off the tram in D'Olier Street where The Irish Times had their offices.

Surprised colleagues greeted him as he made his way to his office cubicle; enquiries about his well-being and health.

Sweeney immediately summoned him to his office. The editor rose from his walnut desk, with a smile on his face, and his hand outstretched. "Welcome back, Tony."

Tony smiled and took his editor's hand. Both men sat.

Sweeney appraised him critically, noting the pale countenance, and the way his top reporter carried himself painfully. A worried tic developed on the older man's face. He decided to give his reporter some good news.

"Got word on that girl you were enquiring about," he said. "She's alive and well."

Tony felt an immediate surge of relief. That was great news.

He spotted the benign look on the older man's face. "What?" he exclaimed, half-annoyed.

"Nothing," Conor grinned back. "Knew that would please you."

"When do you want me back at work?" Tony asked.

Sweeney shrugged. "Want you to take a few days. You're still very pale. When you're fit enough, come back anytime you wish. Do some work from home, if you wish."

Tony nodded. He'd write up some pieces on the Rising from his home. His forced recuperation would help his work.

TONY TURNED OVER IN bed and glanced at the dresser clock. He'd slept for a solid twelve hours since arriving home. He could smell the sea air through the open window. His apartment in Clontarf overlooked the seafront, and Howth Head beckoned off to the left. He had always loved that view over the bay of his native city. The tide was in and the water had that azure blue quality that he loved.

It was through Howth that gun shipments had arrived for both the Irish Volunteers and the Irish Republican Brotherhood prior to the Rising. This was partly in response to events in Ulster, where the Ulster Volunteer Force had been arming themselves through gun runs made through the port of Larne, and they were threatening a wave of civil war if Home Rule came to Ireland. In their eyes Home Rule meant Rome Rule. To Protestants that was simply unacceptable.

McAnthony's wounds racked his body as he struggled up out of bed. He ran a bath in his bathroom and prepared his shaving gear. In the kitchen a pot of tea brewed.

Sipping tea, now refreshed, Tony looked out at the sea. He might start writing about the Rising this morning. The urge to hit the typewriter was strong.

His thin fingers danced hesitantly over the type-writer keys as his brain kicked into gear. Good writing and good reporting required clear thought.

He worked all morning.

At mid-day he lit up a cigarette and surveyed his work. He pencilled in some changes and decided to go for a walk.

As he walked towards St. Anne's Park he couldn't help noticing the surveillance by British intelligence was still in place. The park was one of those places in Dublin where you could escape the pressures of city living. It was quite extensive with large areas of green grass and an avenue that cut right through the centre of it. Rose gardens were tended to near the seafront side, and council horticulturists and gardeners kept a loving hand on the work. Giant trees were in full bloom, as summer approached. Strolling through the park, Tony noticed that the surveillance team had dropped well back. That made sense. In the wide open spaces they would stand out like lighthouses on a foggy night. The afternoon sunshine had brought women into the park with their babies, and here and there families had picnics. The scene made Tony yearn for a family life of his own.

He could remember childhood picnics as a child. Childhood had been an exciting time. The wonder of new places - the memories seared into his brain. The waterfall at Powerscourt, the haunting beauty of the Wicklow Mountains, the rugged coastlines around the southeast in places like Wexford and Waterford. The ethereal beauty, and haunting landscapes of Kerry and Cork, and the white-washed houses and brick walls of Galway and Sligo were seared into his mind.

He remembered his father as a taciturn man who introduced his son to hunting. His father had been somewhat flamboyant, often dressed in tweeds like a country squire. His mother had been a complete opposite, vivacious, good-looking, and very funny. His father had had an adventurous younger life, circumventing the globe as a merchant seaman, before settling down to practice law back in Dublin.

A bit like Conor Sweeney. He had met his wife in Dublin when he defended a case she brought to the courts over a domestic matter.

When they died he was grief-stricken. It changed his outlook of life, and hardened him. He began taking more risks in life. Work became an obsession. He volunteered for the jobs nobody else would touch, but his dedication to his craft saw him through the worse of times, and helped to mould him into the type of journalist he had always admired.

His walk had taken him deep into St Annes, and he realised he'd gone further than he would have wished. His wounds were still healing. He'd pushed himself too far. With a sigh he turned to retrace his steps.

It was a long walk back.

TONY SIPPED HIS TEA and cast a critical eye over the writing he'd laboured to produce all afternoon.

He wrote about the signatories and their personal lives away from revolutionary politics and armed rebellion. He talked about how the students of Padraig Pearse had revered the man and of how even his bearing under captivity had impressed his British captors. He described the poetry of Pearse, written in both Irish and English.

He spoke too, through his writings, of the sculptures completed by Willie Pearse. His writings revealed how both the Pearse brothers had been involved with teaching, and that four of the signatories had been teachers.

His writings captured the souls of the men who had given their all in pursuit of Irish freedom. As the afternoon wore on, he made himself a strong cup of tea and he lit up a cigarette.

He wasn't to know it then, but his writings had shown a nationalistic streak that the British authorities had picked up on.

The orders went out: "Lift him."

CHAPTER 6

DUBLIN. DAYS LATER.

Though the long summer days of June were here, the weather was proving quite wet. Rain slanted over the haphazard shaped rooftops of the city and the sky was gloomy and dark.

Angela found herself thinking of the journalist she had met in the closing stages of the GPO fighting. He had stirred a romantic interest in her heart that she had never felt for another man. He had impressed her with his wit and his daunting courage in accompanying the rebels into the thick of the fighting. He had none of the bravado that some of the younger fighters displayed, or even some of the older ones.

He had struck her as being handsome. A clipped Dublin four accent. Smooth shaven with green shamrock eyes. She knew he'd had a close shave with death; she'd known both men that had been killed who had been chatting with McAnthony before the shell exploded.

She'd first met the journalist face to face when Michael Collins had asked her to look after that young fella over there. Collins had been quick on the scene, quickly checking for vitals on all three men, and moving McAnthony away from the carnage.

She sensed that the British had made a grave mistake in shooting the rebels. They were making martyrs of the men and arousing sympathies even in America. She also sensed the undercurrent of change within the Irish people themselves. From a position of very anti-rebellion attitudes they had embraced the ideal and cause of those fighters who had taken part in the Rising. There was open talk against the

British and plenty of raw anger. Pictures of the dead began appearing in public places, in shop-windows, in homes, on Victorian street poles. The names were whispered whenever Irish people gathered. Pubs, church yards, Gaelic and hurling matches, street corners, schools, doctor's waiting rooms, and on the trams. Irish folk began humming republican tunes and wearing rebel badges and were, at last, openly rebelling against English imperialism.

Perhaps Pearse had been right? Perhaps the seeds of doubt would take years to fester within the Irish people before they arose as a nation en-masse against the forces of the Crown, but with each execution in the Castle, Irish attitudes were hardening.

The Cumann ordered Angela back to Dublin. There was still a lot of work to do. When the prisoners were released from their captivity in England, the struggle would renew itself. In the meantime the women of theCumann had to prepare for the day when once again their services may be needed.

The Cumann had attended 'Month's Mind' masses for the slain leaders of the rebellion. The masses were held in Church Street - a parish where the priests of the diocese had aided the rebels by hearing their last confessions.

The newspapers in Dublin were back to their heavy war reporting. Angela kept her eye on the Times, but saw no by-line with the name of McAnthony. But then towards the end of July a series of articles appeared about the rebellion in conjunction with British calls for an inquiry, and Angela knew McAnthony had lived through his ordeal. Towards the end of July another headline appeared which sealed the fate of Roger Casement - Sentenced to be hanged.

The British were still exacting a measure of revenge. The repercussions of the Rising were savage. Birrell, the Chief Secretary of Ireland, had been forced to resign.

Angela used some of her extensive city contacts to find out about McAnthony. She learned he had recovered well from his wounds and was back working, and by chance learned he would be at the Abbey this coming Friday for a Yeats play - Kathleen ni Houlihan. He had told her in the siege at the GPO that sometimes the Times used him as a theatre critic, though his forte was political analysis.

Angela smiled to herself. It had been awhile since she'd attended the Abbey. Friday would break that abstinence.

She'd contact Lucy to secure complicity in her plan.

"ROME DOES NOT WANT us directly involved in this thing, John.

Troy had been summoned to the Archbishop's residence on foot of the letter he had sent regarding the rebel leaders. The Archbishop had taken his sweet time getting back to him; the rebels had already been shot two months ago, and it was now the middle of a very wet summer. Rain slanted down on the haphazard shaped roof-tops of Dublin City, and the panes of glass in Tuite's house were misted over. Archbishop Raymond Tuite had a forceful presence, a florid face and grey inquisitive eyes. He occupied a palatial house in the heart of Drumcondra, with well manicured gardens out front and tight clipped lawns. The houses were quite Victorian in style. Troy had been shown to the drawing room; his jacket taken, and offered tea and buttered scones, before Tuite joined him.

"Did they say that, Ray?"

Tuite grinned. "Not in so many words, but you know what they're like. Between you and me, I spoke with some of our people in England about this mess and they had some surprising things to say about this whole scenario."

"Like what?"

Tuite was thoughtful, before he continued speaking. "There a lot of very unhappy establishment figures in London who would like to do a Pontius Pilate on this whole Irish problem, but they're afraid if they give up Ireland, they'll have to give up a lot more of their Empire."

"That's interesting," Troy commented, swallowing the last of his scone and taking a sip of his tea. "I wonder what the rebels would make of that?"

"It's important they don't know how close they've come, Father. If they even suspect it, this anarchy will continue for a long time. None of us wants to see that."

Troy remained silent, thinking. Since the executions he had noticed a change, not just among his own parishioners, but also among the Irish people generally. Troy sensed that the writing was on the wall for Redmond's Home Rule Party.

If Sinn Fein didn't emerge with a clear mandate to rule in the next general election, John Troy would be a very surprised man. It was palpable in the very air. People wanted a change. They wanted their country free.

Tuite broke in on his reverie. "What are you thinking?"

"The next elections."

"Redmond's party will swing it."

"I'm not so sure of that, Ray?"

The Archbishop nearly choked on his scone. He was a man with the shape of a pencil; wisp thin, a lean face and cold grey eyes. Tuite was now in his sixties. "You're not seriously telling me, John, that Sinn Fein will pick up the mandate."

Troy just looked at him.

"Good God, man," said Tuite, frowning heavily. "How could you think that?"

Troy shrugged. "It's just a feeling, Ray. It's a sense I'm getting whilst I'm working the parish."

Now it was Tuite's turn to remain silent. He refilled both their cups from the teapot and sighed heavily. "Bishop O'Dwyer of Limerick had some scathing remarks to say about the executions, as you've no doubt heard by now?" Tuite said, sipping his tea thoughtfully. "You're the one working the ground, John. I trust your judgement on this one, though I hope you're wrong."

"Don't you want a free Ireland, Ray?"

"What Irishman doesn't," he replied. "But it's the cost that worries me. The bloodshed. The church has never approved bloodshed. You know that."

That was the hard part to reconcile, thought Troy, draining his teacup. Men like him and the Archbishop had taken vows to support the teachings of Jesus Christ. It didn't leave a lot of room for manoeuvre. Not when people died, often harshly. He said nothing further, but stood as the housemaid brought his coat. As he left he glanced at the Archbishop's face, which was still looking shell-shocked at the younger priest's remark.

Could Sinn Fein really pull it off at the next election?

ENDA MCFRY WAS ALSO wondering the same thing. As a man who always had his pulse on the heart of the country, he sensed that the influence of the Home Party was waning.

Like his wife, McFry worked as a lecturer in Trinity College Dublin. His field was socio-economics, and he published work frequently to certain periodicals and newspapers. Like many of his peers, McFry was proud of his Irish blood and yearned for the day when Ireland would be truly free. Free to decide on its own governance and its own foreign policy. The world was changing and small countries like Ireland wanted their independence. McFry was astute enough to realise that this might mean a blood sacrifice. Better to let the streets run with rivers of blood than to submit lamely to a foreign yolk. Sure wasn't that what the fight in Europe was all about? He knew in his heart that things had to change, and he knew he was part of a huge, unstoppable underground movement to bring about that exact change. He could sense the mood in the people. He could see the changes on a cultural level too - in the literature and poetry currently in vogue, in the theatre halls the length and breadth of the country told through

Irish plays and folklore, and even in the dancehalls, in particular with Irish dancing and ceili music.

He figured it was a good time to be Irish.

McFry had felt nationalistic leanings all his life, but when he was fourteen years of age, those feelings had crystallized into a solid form. Growing up, he'd been part of the scouting movement, that rich body first set up by Lord Baden Powell, and he'd loved every minute of it, even the mundane drill. He could still see himself in the green shirt bedecked with various badges, his blue trousers secured with a scout belt that could double as a bottle opener, his white lanyard which held a whistle that was tucked from sight in his left breast pocket, the green and white neckerchief that was secured by a woggle, his beret with another badge, and the highly polished black shoes.

The shoes of course were replaced by sturdy mountain boots if they were out hiking, and Enda was always hiking. If he wasn't hiking, he was camping out in the elements in places like Powerscourt in Wicklow and the Pine Forest.

His work in higher education, institutes and colleges always having a leaning towards new trends and ideas, had cemented further his nationalism ideals. On the day of the Rising he had been due to attend the Abbey Theatre for a showing of Cathleen ni Houlihan - the play written by William Butler Yeats and Lady Gregory.

He remembered the day when he was a student himself, and the question was put to the class: What would you die for? Most had answered family or friends, and one lad had said his faith.

Only Enda had said his country.

Even at that early stage of his life it was a telling comment, and one which might come to fruition.

He didn't know it at that stage but his life was on the line.

CHAPTER 7

SEVERAL WEEKS WENT by.

Tony's wounds had healed well. His series of articles about the Rising had been

received well. Most newspapers had returned to their heavy World War One reporting.

An enquiry into the Rising was underway.

July brought heavy casualties to the Sons of Ulster. The Somme was bloody and bruising.

The news from the front was terrible.

DUBLIN WAS FULL OF walking wounded.

Prior to the Rising, it was seen as an escapist city, a beautiful city in which to escape the horrors of the war. Courting couples walked hand-in-hand along the streets. Dublin was known as the second city of the British Empire, although by 1916 many of its streets were in gentle decline.

Perhaps it was the sight of the walking wounded and men without limbs that provoked Irish fury whenever talk of Irish conscription raised its ugly head.

Conscription was the new enemy.

THE ARRIVAL OF THE telegram boy heralded bad news for Minnie McGuire.

He waited for her signature and silently handed her the message. His dark eyes betrayed sympathy, but his steps were hurried as he turned back towards his bike. He wanted to be out of earshot before he heard that first cry, which he had heard a thousand times before, and which never failed to pierce the heart.

He was pushing furiously on the pedals when he heard the scream behind him. He shut his eyes and stepped harder on the pedals.

Behind him Minnie's screams had brought her daughter running and neighbours out from neighbouring flats. It was a close-knit community so help was always on hand.

But Minnie had received a double blow. The news was very bad. Both her husband and son had been killed on the Somme. In the space of two minutes her whole world had been turned upside down, and she had aged ten years in the flicker of a heartbeat.

The telegram boy didn't look back.

TROY WAS JUST BACK from a hospital visit when word reached him of Minnie's trouble.

He had spent the afternoon in Temple Street Hospital giving a boy of ten the last rites. The lad had pneumonia - a killer Dublin disease.

When he heard of Minnie's trouble he sighed deeply. His face was troubled as he left the Pro-Cathedral office. The office sold mass cards and other religious trinkets - holy medals, books about St Anthony and St Jude, rosary beads, religious pamphlets.

The atmosphere in Minnie's tenement flat was subdued, hushed. People milled about, but spoke softly. They moved with deference. Soft laughter intermingled with the sound of tears. Folk always gathered at wakes; friends and relations reunited under a common banner that death always brought.

Troy approached Minnie in her sitting room, where most of the women were sitting in comforting poises. The men were sipping whiskey out in the kitchen. No doubt they were discussing politics or sport.

"Sorry for your troubles, Minnie," he said, sympathetically.

She seemed to brighten when he appeared, but her voice when she spoke was harsh and strained. "Oh, Father Troy, how could God do this to me? How...how?" she sobbed.

"Now Minnie," one of her cronies said, "don't be going upsetting yourself," laying a comforting, and craggy hand on her shoulder.

Troy had done this a thousand times. He spoke softly, soothingly. He stated that nobody knew the ways of the Lord. He accepted the sandwiches thrust at him, but ate sparingly. He took the glass of whiskey offered to him. He mixed it with lemonade. And sipped sparingly.

Where ever death appeared drink also put in an appearance. It was the Irish way. Drink had always been an Irish person's crutch in times of trouble. He realised it would be rude to refuse.

And, besides, he liked the odd drop!

IT WAS A STRANGE FUNERAL in many ways.

Because of the nature of war, Minnie's husband and son were both buried were they fell, and there were no coffins in the cathedral to indicate the presence of death.

Minnie was accompanied to the church with her daughters, and all were dressed in black. They had arrived by black horse drawn carriages which were now patiently biding the end of the proceedings outside.

Troy had his back to the congregation as he led the parishioners through the rites of the mass. The Pro-Cathedral was only a stone's throw from Sackville Street and the General Post Office where Padraig Pearse had announced the proclamation only a few months before. It was also known to Dubliners as Saint Mary's church and was the episcopal seat of the Roman Catholic Archbishop of Dublin and Primate of Ireland. It had been built over a townhouse once owned by Lord Annesley on the junction of Marlborough Street and Elephant Lane. Externally the church was built in a Greek style, whilst within had a heavy Roman influence.

Even though it wasn't a full cathedral in the same sense as Christchurch, the new structure completed in 1825 came to be seen as a symbol of the Irish nationalist spirit at a time in history that followed the end of the Penal Laws which had forced Catholicism underground. That the church had survived this onslaught was a testament to the people. Daniel O'Connell, the leader of Irish nationalism at the time and the first Roman Catholic elected to the British House of Commons had attended a High Mass in the Pro-Cathedral four years after it was built following the granting of Catholic Emancipation. In 1849, when O'Connell died his remains were laid in state in the Pro' - a friendly term used by Dubs to describe the cathedral.

The Pro' had seen a number of funerals since. High up in the choir loft at the back of the Pro', the

Palestrina boy's choir were singing the Missa Papae Marcelli. The strong tones helped to lift the spirits of the mourners. Spiritual music could have that effect, Troy had noticed, his own spirit entranced by the beautiful music rafting down from the choir loft.

Troy used the occasion to talk about the importance of standing up against tyranny. He emphasized that such ideals weren't a waste of one's life, but could lay the foundations to a more peaceful existence based on democracy. He said that Minnie's husband and son had fought for a higher cause and that their sacrifice was something to applaud and celebrate.

After the church services the family went to a local establishment that served the obligatory soup and sandwiches for such occasions. Troy went back to his work. He had a busy schedule this week that included visits to the Mater Hospital and Mountjoy prison. If anyone had told him at the time that one day he'd be an inmate at the prison, he'd have laughed aloud. Sadly just such a fate awaited him.

CHAPTER 8

DUBLIN WAS THE CAPITAL city of Ireland, but in many ways it was like a small town in rural Ireland, a place where people regularly bumped into people that they knew. Rebellion aside, the city until relatively recently had been the most popular after London for soldiers taking a few days furlough. Edwardian and Victorian influences were still evident in some well to do city areas, especially around Merrion Square and out towards Ballsbridge. The main street of the capital - Sackville Street - boasted a pillar dedicated to Nelson. The city itself was split into two, and one was either a northsider or a southsider depending on which side of the River Liffey one resided in. Grafton Street was like a mecca for Dubliners, and a place where people often met. It was where Tony met Angela quite by chance late one Saturday evening. They grinned like schoolkids when they spotted one another. Tony's smile widened as he addressed her.

"You escaped, Angela?"

Angela smiled coyly. "Yes...yes, I did," she replied. "And how about you? When I last saw you, you were on a stretcher. How's your shoulder and back?"

"On the mend," he grinned. "Thanks to you. You stemmed a lot of the blood."

"Least I could do," she grinned back. "I heard you got picked up eventually?"

He nodded soberly. "They released me from the Castle, but picked me up afterwards. Sent me to Britain for a while, and just as they were moving the lads to a new camp at Frongoch they released me. Guess they weren't happy I gave their surveillance the slip."

"They have some neck," she exclaimed vehemently, the sudden passion of her words surprising him with the intensity of her feelings. "Did you see how they treated Pearse, Connolly and the others?"

"I saw," he said, sadly. "They died for a free Ireland."

"And we'll carry on their fight," she exclaimed.

"That was the sentiment of the men in England. Collins, de Valera, Griffith."

"It's unstoppable," she said. She flicked a strand of her auburn hair from her eyes.

"I'm writing more revolutionary stuff."

"Are you? Isn't that a little dangerous for you, Tony?"

He shrugged. "We all have to do our bit."

"Cultural nationalism meets militarism," she said, a smile twisting the corners of her lips.

"Yeah," he said, smiling back. "Something like that." He paused, then added: "I was heading towards Grafton Street for some coffee. Like to join me?"

"I'd love to," she smiled. "The Hibernian dining rooms?"

"Why not," he smiled back.

They strolled up Sackville Street together. People bustled by, busy with their lives. The tide was in on the Liffey. Trams scooted by, and horse drawn carriages. Young boys stood on street corners selling newspapers: The Irish Times, Freeman's Journal, Irish Independent.

They found a secluded corner in the Hibernian - the renowned Dublin coffee shop. They sipped quietly for a few moments, relaxed in one each other's company, the silence being neither awkward nor unwelcome.

"So," she smiled.

"So," he said, meeting her level gaze. She had stunning eyes, he thought. He was going to ask her out. He could feel the desire within him. He wondered how to go about it in the best fashion, and then plunged ahead regardless. "So," he said again.

"I was wondering, Angela..."

"Yes," she said, softly, guessing with that woman's intuition what was coming, and smiling modestly to encourage him.

"Are you spoken for, or what?" he finally blurted.

She smiled again. She smiled a lot. "Why, Tony McAnthony, are you propositioning me?" She took a sip of her coffee.

"Yeah, why not." He grinned back. "Dinner tonight. Perhaps a play in the Abbey. How about it?"

She paused, before replying. "That would be really nice, Tony."

McAnthony smiled with delight. "Great," he said. "I'll meet you at the pillar at seven." He drained his coffee cup. "What are your plans for the rest of the day?"

"Shopping," she replied. "And yours?"

"I've got to head for the office," he said. He lit up a cigarette.

"You like smoking?" she observed.

"Occupational hazard," he grinned back. "Nearly every hack I know smokes."

"Hacks?"

"Sorry...journalists."

He helped her with her coat, and they left the coffee shop together. He slipped his arm casually around her as they strolled back down Grafton Street. He left her outside Brown Thomas, with a slight peck on the cheek, and promised to see her later.

"TONY MCANTHONY?"

The harsh command interrupted his train of thought on the way back to his office on D'Olier Street. Two men had accosted him, accompanied by armed British soldiers.

Tony looked up startled. He stopped. Nodded.

"You're under arrest."

"What for?"

"Rebellious acts."

The taller of the two reached forward and hand-cuffed him before he could object further. Tony was simply too astonished to resist.

"This is outrageous," he spluttered. "On whose authority are you acting?"

"We have our orders," the smaller man said, and taking his arm led him towards a vehicle parked near the kerb. They bundled the reporter into the back of the vehicle, and began driving towards Richmond Barracks.

THE INTERROGATOR WAS a hatchet faced Englishman. His voice was harsh as he addressed McAnthony.

Harsh lighting protruding from the ceiling blinded Tony as he sought to keep awake. It was now twelve hours since his arrest. Angela would think he'd stood her up. They had been questioning him relentlessly for hour after hour. He was ravenous: they hadn't provided any food since his arrest. The interrogator's harsh voice again intruded on his thoughts: "Again I ask what were you doing in the GPO?"

"My JOB," he stressed again.

"What prior knowledge had you about the Rising?"

"None."

The interrogator laughed harshly. "Come now, Tony. You don't really expect us to believe that...do you?"

"It's the truth."

"How well did you know the signatories?"

"Not well."

"Can you shoot?"

"Shoot?"

"Rifles. Pistols."

"Yes. I can shoot."

The Englishman smiled coldly. "Where did you learn that skill then, mate? The Volunteers?"

McAnthony scowled. "As a boy. I used to hunt."

"Hunt what?"

"Rabbits. Wildlife."

The Englishman was taking copious notes. He jabbed the pen towards the journalist. "What kind of weapon did you use in the GPO?"

"My pen," McAnthony growled, growing weary of the questioning.

"Huh?"

McAnthony grinned coldly. "Yeah," he said, "I stabbed a few soldiers with my nib."

The Englishman wrote 'stab' with no qualifier. He snapped his notebook shut.

"When do I get out of here?" McAnthony asked, his gaze sweeping up to meet the eyes of his tormentor.

The man didn't reply. He walked towards the door and left silently. The click on the other side made the young journalist wince.

TO SAY CONOR SWEENEY was hopping mad would be an understatement. He was furious.

He had qualified as a journalist more years ago than he cared to remember, but the one thing, which had been drilled into him during his early years, was the notion of the Freedom of the Press. He didn't suffer fools gladly, but when one of his top journalists was implicated in a plot of which he knew nothing, then Conor Sweeney's blood was apt to boil.

He didn't always agree with McAnthony's views, but he did like the man. He recognised in the work of his younger colleague that rare breed of talent that was so hard to find these days - a top reporter who was fearless in nosing out news.

Sweeney felt a pain in his left arm and shoulder, and he knew intuitively that the stress of the situation was getting to him. His job was a pressure filled one, without these extra headaches.

He reached for the telephone and dialled a number for the British Embassy in Ballsbridge.

THE VOICE ON THE OTHER end of the line was quintessentially British. It came across as very upper crust, with a hint of London arrogance, and the stiff upper lip that the British were renowned for.

"A reporter, you say?"

"Yes, one of my top journalists," Sweeney said impatiently.

"And you're the editor of The Irish Times?"

"Yes."

"You'll need to leave this with me. I need time to check this."

"Don't take all day about it then," Sweeney said, and abruptly hung up the telephone.

He tapped the edge of his desk. Annoyed. Impatient.

SLUMPED IN A PRISON cell, Tony McAnthony was also annoyed. He had been banged up. Angela would think he'd stood her up. He had no way of getting word to her. He didn't know what the British were planning for him. False accusations had been levelled at him.

He almost wished he had taken up arms during the 1916 rebellion. He scowled at the wall in front of him.

SHE WAS GROWING COLD standing at the pillar.

Nelson's Pillar dominated Sackville Street. To the left of the GPO when facing outwards from the post office, it towered as a symbol of British dominion over the main street of the land. The street itself was fashionable, with trams lines running north and south, and green leaved trees in the centre. Victorian light poles were spaced evenly, and many of the facades lining both sides of the street were Georgian in appearance.

Angela wondered had she made a mistake. He had said seven, hadn't he? She was starting to get annoyed. Had she mistaken his character? By seven thirty she knew he wouldn't be there. She delayed moving, aware of other people waiting for their dates. She felt sure they would know she'd been stood up.

She thought of McAnthony's smile and realized something must have happened to change his plans. She moved away. A week later, a stranger turned up on her doorstep.

"I'm Conor Sweeney!"

Angela looked at the ebullient figure that had turned up at her doorway and liked him immediately. "Did Tony send you?"

"He stood you up last week?"

Angela blushed. A scarlet colour appeared on her high cheekbones. "What happened to him?"

"He was arrested by British intelligence agents."

"But why," she protested. "He had no hand in the Rising."

"I think they've gathered that by now. Don't worry. We're doing everything we can to get him released, but they've shipped him to Frongoch in

Wales. It may be a few days before he is home." He tossed her the Irish Times. "We're bringing pressure to bear," he pointed out, motioning towards the newspaper.

She spread the newspaper. The by-line was by Sweeney himself.

RENOWNED IRISH JOURNALIST IM-PRISONED IN FRONGOCH

CALLS FOR RELEASE

AN EXCLUSIVE REPORT BY CONOR SWEENEY

She scanned the report and looked at Sweeney who winked in return. She suddenly realised she had not offered him anything. "I'm forgetting my manners," she said. "Can I get you a cup of tea, or perhaps something stronger?"

"Tea's fine, miss."

He watched her as she put the kettle on the stove. She was, he thought, a fine catch of a woman. No wonder his ace reporter was smitten. "Tony tells me he met you during the Rising? In the GPO?"

"Yes."

"It must have been dangerous?"

"I'm a nationalist, Mr Sweeney. It was my duty to be there."

"Conor, please."

"You sound like you think a woman's place is in the home, Conor?" She filled two cups, and handed him one.

Sweeney smiled. "Not necessarily," he agreed with her. "That's just me with my old fashioned hat on. Don't mind me."

"I won't," she smiled back.

"Are there many women like yourself...fighting for what they believe in?"

"Lots," she explained. "Countess Markievicz...you've likely heard of her. Margaret Skinnider. Kathleen Clarke. Many others."

"Interesting," he commented.

"Are you married, Conor?"

"I am. Her name is Mary. We have four children. Grown up now," he added reflectively.

"And your wife...what does she do?"

"She writes...children's stories, things like that. She also has a knack for cartooning, and sells a lot of drawings. She also travels a lot."

"Sounds like a busy woman?"

Conor sipped his tea and took a chocolate biscuit from the tin she had placed beside him. He toyed with it for a moment before continuing: "Yeah, she keeps pretty busy. With the children all grown she has a lot more time on her hands to pursue her interests."

"Have you heard of Ingridhne na hEireann?"

"No. Who are they?"

"The Daughters of Ireland," she translated for him. "They meet on week nights...and teach children Irish...storytelling...you should tell Mary. She might be interested."

"She might," he agreed slowly. "It sounds political though?"

"Does that bother you?" she countered. A grin had appeared on her face, as though she were about to deliver a lecture on women's suffrage movements.

"No," said Sweeney cautiously.

"You sure?"

"I'm sure."

"Another cuppa?" she suggested.

He agreed with alacrity. He was beginning to realise there was more to Angela O'Sullivan than met the eye. She was an interesting conversationalist. Sweeney was fascinated. As a journalist first and foremost it appealed to his inner sense of curiosity to listen to Angela as she described how the various women movements nationwide were contributing to the new sense of Irish nationalism that was sweeping the country.

By the time he donned his hat, Conor Sweeney had a much clearer perspective on nationalism than at any other time in his life. And he also felt something new; a pride...a pride in being Irish.

"YOU'RE LATE HOME," she scolded. "Your dinner's gone cold."

Mary Sweeney was a businesslike woman, with an indolent air, and a whiplash voice that could at times sound like a sergeant-major's on a parade ground. "Where have you been anyway?"

"You won't believe this," he said, "but I've been talking to this fascinating woman all afternoon."

"You're right," she sniffed. "I don't believe you. Have you been drinking?"

He scooped her up in his arms and kissed her.

She giggled like a schoolgirl. Her husband was nothing if not ebullient. He had always had that playful streak. It was one of the things she had fallen for when they first started dating as teenagers. Mary Sweeney was now the wrong side of fifty, but her face looked younger. Though her voice could be sharp, her manner wasn't. She was a slim woman, with pale green eyes and a thoughtful curve to her oval face. It was a face that smiled a lot because Conor made her so happy. She smiled at him now and said: "So, who was this wonder woman?"

"Her name, my darling, is Angela O'Sullivan. She's dating Tony."

"Tony McAnthony?"

Conor sniffed. "How many other Tony's do we know?"

"None, come to think of it," she replied. "So Tony has a new woman in his life? What's she like?"

"Enchanting, my dear. But she's also a rebel."

"A rebel?"

"Yes...one of those...an Irish rebel. That's how they met. In the GPO during the Rising."

"How enchanting?" she commented. "I suppose she's a battle-axe?"

"On the contrary, my dear. She's a very beautiful woman with guts and intelligence to boot. A rare combination in a woman, wouldn't you agree?" There was an impish look in his eyes as he goaded his wife.

"Watch it, buster," she warned.

"HE SHOULD NEVER HAVE been arrested."

Sword eyed the hatchet faced Englishman who had conducted the interrogation on Tony McAnthony. He was furious. They had already had enough bad press over the executions. Hatchet face flushed, his features going beet-red in suppressed rage and when he spoke his words came out in a snarl. "He was with the rebels in the GPO."

"So?" sniffed Sword disdainfully.

"So what was he doing there?"

"What did he tell you he was doing there?"

"He said he was doing his job."

"And didn't you believe him?"

"No."

"Why not?"

"Because he's Irish," snarled hatchet face. "Isn't that enough?"

"No, Major, it's not. Don't you realise the trouble this has caused? Do you not realise how much we need the newspapers on our side? This Rising has caused enough bad feeling without making enemies of the people supporting our stance in this. Where's McAnthony now?"

"He's not here," the sullen voice replied.

"Where's is he?"

"We shipped him to Frongoch."

"What?"

"Frongoch...in Wales."

"I know where it is, Major," Sword ground out. He slapped a hand to his forehead. The situation had just gone from bad to worse. He gave the hatchet faced Major a scathing look and left the room. He'd have to go through London to get the journalist released now. He cursed softly. Why was life always so fucking difficult? Why couldn't thing be easy...uncomplicated...just for once? He felt the mood for a drink coming on, but he dispelled the thought. He had much work to do.

LONDON WASN'T HAPPY.

Sword had known they wouldn't be, and he felt like them telling them: "Hey, don't shoot the messenger." They were very hostile when he made the telephone connection to London and they demanded to know who had been responsible for this mess.

"Major Henry Jones," said Sword, referring to Hatchet Face, pronunciating each syllable and trying hard to keep the obvious glee out of his voice. Hatchet Face was about to get a nasty shock - courtesy of London's displeasure and ire.

"Does he realise the headache he has given us?" the voice from London asked.

"You'd have to ask him that, sir."

"We will, Major Sword. Believe me we will. If the man can't handle a simple intelligence job in Dublin, then perhaps he'd be better off in the trenches in France. We need all the help we can get out there."

"I'm sure you do," Sword said in a non-committal tone.

The London voice sighed. "You'll need to leave this with us...if you're talking with Jones tell him to start shipping his bags."

"You're shipping him to France?"

"Yes, Major.

The phone line went dead.

MICHAEL COLLINS WAS surprised to see Tony McAnthony coming through the gates of Frongoch, but he approached the journalist with a broad smile of welcome on his face.

"Here for an exclusive?" he queried, shaking hands with the journalist.

Tony shook his head. "No. Same reason as the rest of you...I was arrested in Dublin the other day...questioned at the Castle...and then shipped here."

The smile disappeared from Collin's face. "In heaven's name why? Didn't you tell them you were just doing your job?"

"I did," McAnthony said. "They didn't believe me."

Collins whistled. "That's the Brits for you...there's many a man here had no hand in the Rising...but they're still locked up. There was a country wide sweep...anyone remotely connected with the Volunteers was lifted."

Tony glanced around the camp. Huts spaced at different angles, mud-baths between them.

Collins took his bag from him and said: "I'll help you get settled."

"What's it like here?"

"Ain't no boy's camp," Collins advised. "Place is full of rats."

McAnthony made a face.

"Don't worry," Collins replied. "You get used to it. Any news from home?"

Tony explained how things were developing back home...how people's attitudes had changed since the Rising...the level of support feeding through to outright nationalism in a number of areas.

Collins was very interested in the news from Ireland. He heard the journalist out and then commented: "Pearse was right...the seeds have been sown."

"Did you hear what Yeat's wrote?"

"No. What?"

"He wrote: A terrible beauty is born."

Collins smiled. "The Irish always had the gift of the 'gab', and especially its writers.

"MCANTHONY?"

The men were gathered in the yard for morning roll call when the Chief warder let out his shout. A military type he was renowned amongst the prisoners for his tough, uncompromising attitude to the prisoners. Tony wondered what he had done to raise the man's ire? He spoke up reluctantly.

"Here, sir," he called back.

The man approached him, eying him up and down. "You're Tony McAnthony, the Dublin journalist?"

"Yes, sir."

"Fall out, man. Collect your gear. Report to the guv'nor."

"Any particular reason?"

The warder gave him a baleful look. "You must have powerful friends...you're out of here. You lucky sod."

Tony concealed a grin and turned to return to his cellblock. The men muttered. "Luck to you, lad." Collins whispered an urgent message as he went by. "Give my regards to Ireland, Tony."

He collected his gear, which wasn't much, and was escorted to the governor's office by two warders.

The governor greeted him warmly. "There's been a bit of a mix-up," he explained. "It has come to our attention that you should never have been sent here. Our Majesty's Government wishes to apologise for this mistake. You are free to leave here."

"Just like that," McAnthony commented quietly. "And those other men out there on the parade ground...when will they be released?"

"That's not your concern, Tony. They are being detained at her Majesty's pleasure." He eyed the journalist silently. "May I speak frankly...strictly off the record?"

Tony waved his hand in assent.

"Between you and me...I wouldn't say their stay will be a long one. My guess is most will be out for Christmas."

ADJUSTING TO THE HARSH regime within Frongoch wasn't easy, and Enda McFry was having trouble sleeping at nights. He brooded constantly about his wife Susan, and hoped that she at least might be released soon.

During the day he enjoyed the company of men like Pairic O'Toole and Tadhg O'Sullivan. In many ways they were poles apart but they were united in a love for their country and a huge desire to see Ireland free. McFry was more of a studious individual who devoured books and newspapers like biscuits, but he enjoyed Irish games too, and was often seen with Pairic and Tadhg practicing hurling together. Sometimes he found O'Toole a trifle cold, and he assumed correctly that it was because he was closer to Dev than to Collins. He knew O'Toole to be a fearless fighter for his country, but also a man who hated the violence and the killing associated with the fight and the struggle for Irish freedom.

Tadhg was the opposite; young, brash, confident, and easily influenced by the type of men around him. He was the quintessential Kerryman though, and often had a broad smile on his face. He spoke up now as the trio of men took a break from throwing a ball around: "Lucky sod...that journalist."

"Who?" O'Toole asked.

"McAnthony. Tony McAnthony. Mick told me he was let out this morning."

"He was in the GPO, right?" McFry queried.

"Aye," Tadhg confirmed. "But he had no hand in the scrap."

McFry was thinking of how much he'd like to be on his way home now. He voiced the thought to his companions. "You're right, Tadhg. Lucky sod. Wonder when they'll let us out?"

O'Toole spat on the ground. "When they've decided we've had enough," he declared. "They can't keep hundreds of us locked for ever. It must be costing them a small fortune."

It was an aspect of the affair McFry hadn't considered. He suddenly gave his two companions a wide grin. Perhaps they'd be released for Christmas. The thought was a cheery one.

CHAPTER 9

THE ABBEY THEATRE PLAYED no small part in helping the Irish people develop an indigenous view of their own take on life. Irish plays and folktales and stories were regularly staged that betrayed an emerging sense of national identity.

The Irish Times was to the forefront whenever a new play appeared. Critical, informative, always engaging.

On Friday evening a queue formed early.

Angela was dressed to the nines - and wore a revealing black dress with a light white shawl. The long hot summer days brought the heights of Parisian, London and Milanese fashion into the departmental stores of Dublin, and manifested itself in the elegant evening wear worn by the theatre set that flocked regularly to plays at the Abbey, like elegant, graceful swans in the Green. She had persuaded her friend Lucy to accompany her. As yet there was no sign of Tony, and she hoped her information had been correct. She knew though that he didn't need to queue. He could turn up at the last moment and flash his press identification, and would be admitted with little or no fanfare.

That was one of the little perks of his profession.

The women moved through the foyer, Angela's eyes still scanning the crowd.

Lucy nudged her with a knowing smile. "No sign yet, then."

Angela shook her head, trying to mask her disappointment. The women entered the theatre and the show commenced.

It was during the interval that Angela spotted his familiar face, and she approached him. He didn't see her approach.

"We meet again."

He turned with a slow smile creeping across his features. "Indeed we do," he said. "Indeed we do."

"How's your shoulder?"

"Healing well, thanks to you," he replied. "Are you enjoying the play?"

"Yes. And you?"

He shrugged nonchalantly. "As much as I can when I'm working. When I'm here to critique it, write about it." His eyes were scanning the crowd behind her. "Are you here with somebody?" he asked.

Lucy was approaching them, an impish smile on her face. "So this is your beau," she exclaimed cheekily.

Angela blushed. "Lucy, this is Tony McAnthony. Tony, Lucy."

Tony smiled and shook hands with Lucy Brown Corish. "Any friend of Angela's," he said, "is a friend of mine."

"A charmer too, I see," Lucy smiled, winking at her friend, but liking the journalist's firm handshake.

They made small talk for a few moments, and then Tony announced the play would be starting back. "Perhaps you ladies would take a lift later?"

The ladies nodded their heads and they made arrangements to meet back in the foyer when the play was over.

"SO TONY, THEY RELEASED you from Frongoch?"

Tony had met with the women after the play and had dropped Lucy off at her house on Moore Street. She had chattered all the way. Her good humour and infectious nature had them both in stitches. Tony was still smiling at her antics after she had left his car. He had then driven Angela to her house on the South Circular Road. His car engine was idling as they talked. The canal water beside them flickered light from the Victorian street lamps.

"Thanks to Lucy," Angela replied. "She lived close to the GPO, so it was easy to escape."

"She seems like a good friend to have," he commented. "Is she always so cheeky?"

Angela laughed. "Don't take her too much to heart. She liked you, I could tell. She can be very cheeky, but she has a heart of gold." She paused for a moment and then went serious. "I escaped the effects of the Rising. Others weren't so lucky. Did you see what happened to Pearse?" Her face worked furiously, and he could sense she was close to tears.

He hesitated and then put his arm around her shoulders. The scent of her perfume hit his nostrils, as she snuggled her head against his shoulder. "Easy, Angela," he comforted. "They died for a free Ireland."

"I know," she said, in a small voice. She suddenly seemed very vulnerable. She raised her head and looked into his eyes.

His thin lips joined hers, a soft lingering kiss.

"Oh, Tony," she exclaimed, as their momentary passion faded.

He smiled again at her. "I'll see you to your door," he said, reaching for the door handle. He moved easy around the car, and opened her door for her. He took her arm and escorted her to the door.

They turned to each other. And kissed again.

"When can I see you again?" he asked, as she put the key in her door.

She smiled demurely. "Tomorrow?"

Once again he grinned. "Tomorrow sounds good," he said.

Angela leaned against the door as she entered the hall. She heard Tony's car start outside. She was suddenly pleased she had taken the bull by the horns and gone to the play. Tonight had been a stunning success. Smiling she headed for her bedroom.

Her last thought before sleeping into a sound sleep was: Tomorrow!

GLORIOUS SUNSHINE HIT Dublin the following morning. A Saturday.

True to his word, Tony rolled up his open topped car at lunchtime. Angela had spent the morning preparing a picnic - cold meat sandwiches, fresh fruit that Lucy had brought out to her earlier from the stalls at Moore Street, a flask of soup, and cold drinks.

Lucy had ridden up on her bicycle at ten. Her eyes blazed with curiosity. She brought the fruit into the house, whilst Angela prepared some tea for her friend. The black kettle simmered on the cast-iron stove. They chatted as only women can. "Well," Lucy burst out eventually, "are you going to leave me in suspense. How did you make out with your beau?"

Angela smiled. "Grand."

"Grand?" Lucy exploded. "Are you meeting him again?"

"Later," Angela confirmed.

"And?"

"And what?"

"Give me the details. What happened?"

"Nothing happened."

"Nothing," Lucy said, her face dropping. She looked crestfallen. Angela's heart yielded.

"Well...", Angela began.

"Come on girl, give," Lucy said threateningly.

"Well, we kissed."

Lucy laughed delightedly. "I knew it," she exclaimed. "I just knew it."

"Knew what?" Angela sounded half mad, as though fearful she'd let too much slip. She knew Lucy didn't gossip, but still?

Lucy was still grinning. "I just knew you were both made for each other. I saw the way you were looking at him, and the way he looked at you. The chemistry was there."

"That obvious, huh?" Angela's tone was curt.

"Lighten up, Angela," Lucy persisted, her friendly smile wiping away her friend's fears. "He'll be good for you, Angela. I can sense it. Believe me, I know these things. Sure, what age was I married at? Seventeen. He's got a good job, good looks to boot. Even a car, for heaven's sake. What more do you want? You did good, girl. You're made."

"His job and possessions don't interest me as much as the man, Lucy," said Angela seriously.

Lucy sobered. "I know that, hon'. But these things don't hurt, do they?"

"No. You're right, Lucy. I got lucky."

The two women chatted over a pot of tea, and then Lucy announced she had to go. "Got to go, hon'. There's no rest for the wicked and the work is waiting."

"I'll see you out," Angela said.

They pecked one another on the cheek and Lucy gave her friend some parting advice: "Keep me in the loop, won't you? Let me know what's happening?"

Angela promised.

"A PICNIC?" TONY HAD exclaimed with delight.

"If you don't mind driving," she said.

"With this kind of weather," he commented. "It would be a delight. I like the outdoors, anyway. Do you?"

"Love it," she agreed. "Where shall we go?"

Tony thought for a moment, picking up the picnic basket, and watching as she fetched a shawl in case the weather turned later. He concealed a grin. That was a real Irish trait - expecting the weather to turn at any moment.

"You're grinning?" she accused.

"Am I?" he countered. Teasing her.

"Share the joke," she said.

He explained about the shawl. She smiled. Now it was her turn to tease. "It's not just the weather," she said. "What if our date doesn't work out? You might decide to leave me, make me walk home."

He frowned. "What could give you that idea?"

"Relax. I'm joking."

He wagged his finger accusingly. "Two wrongs..."

"Don't make a right," she finished. "You're right. Forgive my sense of humour."

"Forgiven," he smiled. He thought for a moment. "How does Howth sound?"

"Delightful!" She linked her arm into his. "Shall we?"

"Lets."

ON A CLEAR SUNNY DAY the hill of Howth commanded a magnificent view out over Dublin Bay. They had left the car at the summit and had walked to a quiet spot down near the Bailey lighthouse.

Half of Dublin seemed to be out enjoying the sunshine. Parents and young couples walked together, children squealed as they raced around, and old folk tottered along with dogs at their heels. Out in the bay a few sailboats bobbed gently. Angela looked at Tony as he lounged on the grass, the summer heather in bloom behind him. The soup and sandwiches were gone, and they sipped tea that Angela had brought along in another flask. Tony lit up a cigarette.

"Do you smoke much?" she asked him.

"Now and again," he explained. "I like one with a cuppa." He sipped his tea, liking the strong brew.

"I saw your articles in the Times. About the Rising."

He put his cup carefully on the grass. "What did you think of them?"

"They were good," she enthused. "Inspiring."

He told her about the history of the newspaper, and described the pro-British slant it took in its reporting. She listened with interest, her long slender body stretched on the grass, soaking up the rays of the hot orb in the sky. She put a question to him.

"Why did they publish my Irish slant on the Rising?" he mused aloud, repeating her question. "They know I'm a good reporter. There's always balance." He lifted his cup to his mouth and paused before adding: "Besides I've a good editor in Conor Sweeney." He told her something about Conor.

"He's your friend?" she asked.

"Yes."

"Friends are important," she encouraged. "He came to see me when you were arrested."

"Yes. I know."

"That night at the Pillar...I thought you'd stood me up."

"That was unavoidable," he explained. "That's why I sent Conor to see you."

He reached towards her and brushed a strand of hair from her eyes. "You have beautiful hair," he commented.

She giggled.

"I mean it, Angel. Everything about you is beautiful. I'm going to call you Angel from now - my beautiful little Angel."

She laughed again - self-consciously. "I think Lucy was right about you, Tony. You're a real charmer."

"Only when it matters," he claimed unabashed.

She took up the flask. "More tea?"

"Pour away," he said, holding out his cup. He eyed her over the rim of his cup. "How long have you been living in Dublin, Angel?"

"Ten years. Give or take. I visit home every couple of weeks."

"Kerry, right? What part?"

"Fenit."

"What's that like?"

"Quiet," she replied. "Very peaceful though. My father's retired now from the farm, and Henry - he's my older brother, the eldest - runs the place now."

"Have you a big family?"

"Four brothers. My mother died when I was little."

"I'm sorry," he said. "How old were you then?"

"Six."

"And you remember her, yes?"

"I do. She was a fine woman. How about you, any family?"

He laughed. "No. I'm a lone wolf."

"How about your parents?"

"They're both dead." He paused, before adding. "They died on the Titanic."

"On the Titanic?"

He nodded. "My mother was offered a place on a lifeboat, but she wouldn't leave without my father. From what I could gather they went down together."

"That's sweet," she commented. "Sweet, but sad. She must have loved your father a great deal?"

"I guess she did," he remarked. He was silent and broody for a moment. The loss of the White Star ship, a few short years before, still brought back painful memories.

Angela placed a hand on his knee. "It still hurts, doesn't it?"

"Yes."

"Do you believe in a life after this one, Tony?"

"In God? Sure sometimes."

"So do I," she exclaimed happily. "And believing that...believing that I think you'll meet them again one day...in another world...a better world than this one."

"Sounds too good to be true?"

"I know it does, Tony. But we've got to have faith...don't you agree?"

"Faith's important," he agreed, "but sometimes I'm assailed by doubts. Don't you get those?"

She smiled. "I think we all do," she said simply. "We wouldn't be human otherwise."

WHEN THE MEN FROM FRONGOCH were released there was joy throughout Ireland. Crowds lined the docks as the men arrived home. Christmas 1916 was fast approaching. Bunting and tinsel hung everywhere and churches had built their cribs. Carol singing could be heard in the streets.

But the fight was a long way from being over. Lessons had been learned from the GPO. From now the Irish would bring an irregular aspect to their fight, and would rage a vicious guerrilla war against their oppressors.

No quarter would be given. It was better to die like a man with a gun in the hand, than to live for another moment with the yoke of foreign oppression hanging over the nation.

New leaders had emerged from the ashes of the Rising. Men like de Valera, Michael Collins and Harry Boland would bring a new kind of fighting to the struggle. The key figure in this new type of warfare would be the tall man from Cork - Michael Collins.

TROY WATCHED FROM THE docks as the cheering Irish crowds welcomed the survivors of the Rising home, and he wondered at the fickle nature of people. He remembered the scenes of a very different nature when the men were being shipped off when they were spat upon and set upon. He had no doubt in his mind that some of the same people who had seen these men off in such a fashion were the very same ones who now welcomed these men back with open arms.

Ah, the fickle nature of the Irish, he mused.

As a man of the cloth, Troy wondered about his own sense of euphoria at seeing the return of these rebels. He supposed he was an Irishman first, and a priest second. He knew of other priests through-out the city of Dublin who had directly participated in the Rising, not by taking up guns, but by openly helping those involved.

Throughout Irish history the priests of Ireland had always being caught up in the politics of the country. What they said from the pulpit on a Sunday morning was gospel to the ears of their followers, and their words carried a lot of weight. Indeed in looking back at Irish history, priests had often been directly involved in the violence of uprisings, and the 1798 rebellion in Wexford had been led by clerics, most notably Fr. John Murphy.

A parishioner he knew broke his reverie.

"Surprised to see you here, Father?"

"Why is that, Billy?"

Billy Hannafin grinned and shrugged his builder's shoulders. A stocky man, Billy came from the north inner city, and had a huge family. When he spoke his voice was that of a pure Dub.

"Oh, I don't know," he grinned. "I didn't realise you were a rebel supporter."

"Keep it a secret Billy, would you?"

Billy grinned and whispered. "Don't worry, Father. Your secret is safe with me."

Tony watched the men disembark from the train at Westland Row. His arm was around Angela's shoulders, and on her finger an engagement ring shone. Tony recognised some familiar faces. Harry Boland, Cathal Brugha, and Michael Collins.

Collins spotted him and grinned widely. "How's the lad?" he enquired, in that distinctive West Cork accent.

Tony smiled and shook hands. "Welcome home, Michael. You know Angela, don't you?"

"Sure, didn't I introduce the pair of ye?"

"We're walking out together," Angela explained.

"Courting," Tony added.

"Congratulations," Collins grinned. "Hope I'm invited to the wedding."

Tony was thoughtful. "What now, Mick? Any plans?"

Collins sobered. "The fight goes on," he declared. "We learned some lessons from the 1916 Rising. We won't make that mistake again."

"How's that?" Angela looked interested.

Collins explained. "From here we're going to fight a war of attrition...a guerrilla war. Hit and run tactics."

"It won't be easy," Tony commented. "You'll need lots of luck, and weapons."

"We'll make our own luck. Weapons are always a problem, but we'll get them."

The crowds were beginning to disperse.

Collins promised to keep in touch and wandered off with his friend - Harry Boland.

Tony watched them go, a small smile playing the corners of his mouth.

Angela nudged him. "What are you thinking?"

"Brave guys," he said, nodding at the men. "Comrades in arms."

ANGELA SMILED AS FATHER Troy approached them.

She had met him before. She introduced Tony to the priest. He surprised Tony by seeming to know something about his work.

"Father," Tony acknowledged, shaking hands, surprised by the strength and firmness of Troy's handshake.

Troy indicated the crowd with a sweep of his hand. "They sure are fickle," he observed shrewdly. "Months ago they were probably baying for blood."

Tony laughed. "That's a pessimistic view, Father?"

"Perhaps," Troy said. He eyed the young journalist. "You work for Conor Sweeney, don't you?"

"Yes," said Tony. "Do you know Conor?"

"Aye lad. We often shared a bottle of the hard stuff. Did you get over your wounds...from the Rising?"

"Surprised you know about them?" Tony glanced quizzically at Angela.

"I saw you...at the Castle," Troy explained. "On a stretcher."

"Father Troy tried to save the rebels...he intervened with the British on their behalf," Angela explained to Tony.

Troy's face darkened. "Not with much success, I'm afraid."

"London wanted its revenge, Father...Pearse and them were beyond saving. They were marked down as soon as they signed that proclamation." Tony's words brought a sad smile to Troy's countenance.

"Perhaps," he remarked sadly. "But still...?

Angela placed a consoling hand on the priest's sleeve, surprising both men, with her spontaneous gesture of affection. "You did what you could, Father...some folk did nothing...at least you tried."

Troy's head bobbed up and down. "God's will, I suppose?"

"Padraig Pearse's will," Angela announced passionately. The level of intensity in her words brought a smile, and then open laughter to the two men.

Angela looked in puzzlement at their laughter for a moment, and then joined in. With Christmas approaching good humour was in abundance. She spotted her younger brother climbing from the train and shouted out his name.

"Tadhg?"

The young man grinned and running towards her swept her off her feet. "Hi, sis," he greeted.

"Tadhg," she said, "I'd like you to meet Tony McAnthony...and this gent is Father John Troy."

The young Kerry lad shook hands with both men. His eyes widened when he spotted McAnthony. "Hey, weren't you with us in Frongoch?"

"For a few days," Tony said, recalling the young man now. He hadn't known then he was related to Angela. He remembered the lad playing a game of hurling on the prison yard.

Troy glanced at his watch and wished them luck. He had masses later. Angela explained how she was seeing Tony, and the younger man grinned and said: "This calls for a celebration. Let's find a boozer."

Angela eyed her younger brother with a mock frown. "Some things don't change," she commented wryly, but there was a light brevity in her voice that belied the content of her words.

PAIRIC O'TOOLE WALKED off the gangplank of the ship and his massive shoulders heaved as he breathed the fresh sea air. "Ah," he said with relish. "Fresh Irish air."

Declan Hannafin nudged his brother Ciaran and grinned at the antics of O'Toole. "Free too," he commented.

O'Toole grinned at the pair. "Betcha' life," he agreed. "Can't wait to have a pint. Will you lads join me?"

"Later maybe," Ciaran replied. "We've got to catch up with our family first."

Pairic nodded seriously. "Family first," he stated. "I like that."

"Where will you be later?" Declan asked.

"The Brazen Head, no doubt." Dublin's oldest pub tended to attract those with nationalistic leanings, and it was known for selling a good pint of the black stuff.

THE CROWDS SURPRISED Enda McFry.

He caught sight of Susan who had been released some months before, and he waved. It was hard to get through the enthusiastic people who had turned out in droves to welcome the men home.

The irony of it staggered him. Months before some of this crowd had probably been among those who had seen the prisoners off...but then again perhaps he was being harsh. He was already looking forward to Christmas.

There would be much work to do. Elections were only a year away, and the party would have lots of work for him. A Sinn Fein convention was only months away. He would give it his best shot. His strength lay in his organisational genius, his innate ability when it came to strategy.

Susan caught his eye and waved back.

He took her into his arms immediately and kissed her hard on her lips. She responded in kind. It had been months since they had held one another.

"I'm so glad you're out," she breathed. Her dusky green eyes appraised him.

"Me too," he responded. "Think I've changed?"

"You've lost some weight," she observed. "It suits you."

"I'm still looking forward to a good steak," he laughed.

She laughed with him. "I hope that's not all you're looking forward to?"

"It isn't," he grinned, linking his arm in hers.

"I know just the place," she added.

THE MCFRY'S LIVED IN Rathgar.

In the bedroom she came to him. He reached for her, drawing her body close. She had stripped quickly, her breathing shallow in anticipation. "Hey, what happened to my steak?" he laughed, wasting no time in shedding his own clothes.

"That comes later," she responded. "Right now I want you to carve me up."

McFry laid her gently on the bed, his body folding into hers as he entered her with little foreplay. She moaned, and arched her head back, revealing the soft neck, which he grasped with his teeth. He could smell the lingering perfume in her hair, the scent arousing him further and making him thrust harder between her legs.

She groaned aloud and scratched his back with her long fingernails.

Their movements were now smooth, pulsating. He could feel the rush. He tried holding back for that moment longer, but it was no use. It was months since they had sex - a prison cell in England being no place to indulge your fantasies. They explored one another's bodies like foolhardy teenagers, but each comfortable with the other, revisiting old ground, discovering one another anew.

They made love again and again throughout the afternoon, the afternoon sun bathing their bodies as it crept in through the open drapes. The light brought shadows and fulfilment and they talked when their passions had died down. As the sun bedded down low in the sky he fell into a light sleep. She moved without waking him, throwing her bathrobe around her body.

Moments later he stirred. The sizzle coming from the kitchen meant she had been well pleased with their afternoon's work. An aroma of mushroom, onion and steak reached him. He stared up at the ceiling. He'd have to paint that soon.

God, it was good to be home.

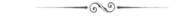

CHRISTMAS 1916 PROVED to be a happy one for Tony.

He remembered spending other Christmas's alone, but his courtship with Angela was helping to bring him back into a family circle. He had accompanied her to Kerry for the festivities, and he had met some of her family for the first time. Tadhg also went home for the Christmas. Jonjo, her father, had gripped him by the hand whilst looking him over. He could tell a lot about a man from his handshake. The handshake was firm, strong. Jonjo had exchanged a look with his eldest son, Henry, who had also shaken the journalist by the hand. Jonjo winked at Henry, and then glanced back at the journalist. "Tell me lad, do ye box?"

"Box?"

"Oh, father," Angela groaned, rolling her eyes.

Tony smiled in puzzlement.

"Henry here," he said, indicating his eldest son, "does a bit of boxing. We call him Boxer. He's quite a fighter."

Henry grinned and Angela shook a warning finger at her father and brothers. "Don't pay them no never mind," she explained crossly. "They ask every stranger the same question."

Tony surprised them. "I used to fight a bit when I was younger."

Angela looked at him in surprise, and her old man laughed in delight. "In the ring?" he asked.

Henry eyed him anew, taking in the broad shoulders, wondering could he take him. There was a calculating, speculative look in his eyes.

Tony grinned. "In the ring," he confirmed.

Jonjo looked delighted. "This calls for a drink," he enthused. He looked at Henry with a raised eyebrow, and the younger man nodded with an imperceptible nod of his head. "I'll set it up," Jonjo continued. "St Stephen's night...when I've let all the neighbours know."

"Boxing night," Henry quipped.

"YOU SHOULD NEVER HAVE agreed," Angela counselled, though there was a twinkle in her eyes as she said it. "My family like you," she said as they strolled along Fenit beach, after one of the best Christmas dinners Tony had enjoyed in a long time. White frothed waves crashed along the desolate but beautiful beach. They had decided after the meal to go for a long walk. Tony had met many of the neighbours over drinks the previous evening and at Christmas morning mass. Young local boys and girls had entertained the mass with Christmas carols.

Tony had fielded quite a few questions on the up-coming fight. It seemed everyone was looking for-ward to it.

The old man and Boxer had disappeared into the big red haybarn after Christmas dinner. The table had been full of jollity and crackers being opened, with perhaps just a tinge of sadness for family who had passed away. Christmas always brought those bitter-sweet moments. The massive turkey had been killed on the farm only a day or two earlier, the old man wringing its neck in a swift, practiced move-ment. As they strolled along the beach, Tony made a remark to Angela.

She laughed like a schoolgirl at his question. She shook her head, her hair hidden beneath a thick blue woollen hat. "It's not just the prospect of a fight," she explained. "They like you. Didn't you see the atmos-phere around the Christmas table? All the talk...they never open up like that to strangers. Never."

"They're good people, Angel."

"Aye," she agreed.

"I take it your brother can fight a bit?"

"Nobody from hereabouts has beaten him. A man from the north beat him once, but Boxer was feeling under the weather. You'll need to watch out for him...and watch his left hook."

Tony filed the information away. He was willing to bet he'd need every edge to take the lanky farmer tomorrow. There was a quiet air of confidence in the young farmer. Angela was still speaking.

"They'll be working flat out now...getting that ring ready."

"It's nice down here," he added. "Wild, but very beautiful."

"And desolate too, sometimes."

"I like it."

"So do I. I love it, but then I grew up here."

"That must have been an adventure?"

"Things were different back then," she murmured. A shadow crossed her face. "My mother was alive back then"

"You still miss her, don't you?" he asked softly. "How long is it now...ten, twelve years?"

She nodded. The bobbin on her hat looked cute. "This time of the year is always the worst...the memories flood back."

"I know," he said quietly, feeling the sudden urge to take her in his arms and kiss her. Which he did.

They stepped apart after a few moments, breathless, their breathing as ragged as the timeless rocks littering the shore. Their hearts pounded like the surf upon the boulders. White froth moved back and forth with the movement of the tide. An undercurrent hung in the crisp air. They smiled at one another like fools, happy in one another's company, bonded by time and place. Their innate spirits reached out like a tongue of land into the wild Atlantic, as they joined again, and he guided her onto her back on the somewhat wet sand.

Their movements were poetic, not clumsy, and she encouraged him as his hand swept beneath her polo neck and cradled her breast. She sighed deeply.

"Tony, make love to me," she murmured, burying her head in the folds of his neck, clutching him in a tight embrace. The sands shifted beneath her as he took her in the lonely dunes alongside the shingled beach, his frantic movements and thrusts pushing forward like an unstoppable wave, the dunes masking their subtle movements as they united in a white glow of unrelenting passion, as sudden as a storm-break on a bleak shoreline. She cried out as she felt his thrusts deep within her, her cry mingling with that of the seabirds overhead. Nearby a lone seabird sitting on a rocky outcrop, arched its wings, as though suddenly it too had been released, its wings erect and its beak filled with excitement.

They nestled together, only moving to fix their clothes, when the seeping cold from the harsh elements of the Atlantic made their presence known. They smiled again at one another and moved in tandem away from the beach.

Behind them the waves crashed with wild abandon.

THE HANNAFIN BOYS WERE also home for Christmas 1916.

Billy welcomed his two sons with open arms. He had been very worried about them during their enforced incarceration in Wales. Both arrived with those infectious grins, and began by helping out with the usual chores. The tree had to go up, with its tinsel and lights, firewood had to be collected, food, drink. There was much to do in the Hannafin household.

On Christmas Eve as the women finished their chores; peeling the sprouts and the potatoes for the next day, checking the puddings, icing the Christmas cake, boiling the ham and numerous other bits and pieces, the women shared mulled wine between themselves and settled in front of the fire for an evening of craic. The men drank from their porter bottles and many neighbours and relations dropped by.

Declan and Ciaran spoke about their experiences during the Rising and its aftermath, and both were given a hearty welcome home. Their girlfriends, both of whom were blond lassies had joined them for the festivities. Some weren't drinking and wanted to go to mid-night mass in the pro. Most who joined the Hannafins that particular night had at least one drink and joined in the inevitable sing-song and hooley that followed.

TONY CRASHED ONTO HIS back in the middle of the fourth round.

The fight had started well, both men circling around each other, each feinting, parrying, testing the strengths of one another. Onlookers gathered at the ropes, their faces alight with anticipation; their moon faces relishing the prospects as they sipped drinks provided by the host. They had travelled from near and far for this fight. They had appointed Tony with a local manager, a man by the name of Dingle

McGee, who had once fought Jonjo to a standstill, but who had eventually succumbed to the young Kerry fighter in the tenth round. Dingle had warned him about Henry's right hook and Tony had already felt the effects of that wicked right.

It was one of those wicked rights that had floored him in the fourth round.

Up until this moment both men had sparred gamely, neither man giving the other an inch, both giving as good as they got. Tony had caught the Kerryman with a rolling left sucker punch, but the dogged Kerryman had shaken off the effects with a tight grin.

Both men wore thick boxing gloves, and long shorts with light boots. Both wore sleeveless vests.

The referee was counting. "...five, six, seven."

Tony struggled to his feet. He shook his head to clear it. The referee held up a few fingers. "How many?" he asked.

"Three," Tony replied.

"Fight on," the man said, satisfied with Tony's coherence.

Both men circled one another, searching for an opening. They parried blows, ducked and weaved, using the full width of the ring to their advantage. The crowd were enthralled by the contest. In the eight round, Tony managed to swing a wicked right punch that floored the young farmer, catching the man on the point of his jaw, but the Boxer was soon on his feet, a deeper respect in his pale blue eyes. In the ninth, Tony received a cut above the eye that Dingle had to stitch. In the tenth he managed to draw blood from his opponent. Both men had a black eye.

The final two rounds saw both men trading punch for punch, and when the final bell rang, neither man was sure who had won. The judges went into a huddle, arguing amongst themselves. Eventually the ref approached and took both men into the centre of the ring. He lifted the Boxers arm and declared Henry the winner.

The boxers touched one another with their gloves, Tony giving a rueful grin, as he congratulated his opponent. The Boxer grinned back at him and announced: "Hard luck. You were very game."

As Tony retreated to his corner, Dingle handed him a towel. "Hard luck, Tony," he drawled. "You fought well. Nobody has ever taken the Boxer the distance before."

The journalist found commiserations from all quarters, and near the door money was changing hands as bets were settled. Jonjo seemed to have made a packet.

He grinned an apology at McAnthony. "Had to bet on young Henry," he explained. "I've seen him fight. You're the first man ever took him the distance though."

"Some consolation," Tony remarked. "What happens now?"

"Party time," the old man grinned. "A few hot toddies and a bag of ice for the pair of ye and ye'll be right as rain."

Angela grinned at him and he went over to her and put his arms around her. Her forefinger touched his eye. "Is it sore?" she asked. "I told you Henry could fight."

"He's a scrapper all right," Tony confirmed.

"You surprised a lot of folk," she admitted. "Nobody guessed the fight would go the distance."

Tony was beginning to feel the effects. "Let's go back to the house, Angel."

IT WAS DURING THE NEXT two to three years that Tony and Angela's relationship blossomed, both spending a lot of time together, and then when they were separated by work or whatever, both wishing they could have more time together. It wasn't long before they began going away together. Long country weekends to places like the Aran Islands, Sligo, Wexford, Cork, and of course, Kerry. The mountain kingdom, or as some Kerry folk put it, simply the kingdom.

They were so much in love with one another, that it was hard to imagine what could tear them apart, but there were dark horizons ahead, not just for Tony and Angela, but for Ireland as a whole.

CHAPTER 10

TROY'S ATTITUDES TOWARDS events in Ireland had hardened.

They had hardened to such an extent that he sometimes doubted his priestly vocation, and his new militant airs were beginning to rub off the shoulders of higher members of the hierarchy, who tended now to view him with some suspicion.

He no longer had the ear of the Archbishop, and was only summoned to Tuite when no other alternative was possible. As for Tuite himself, he was listening to older, wiser counsel, who counselled advice to distance himself from his radical young priest.

Troy wasn't sure when the change within himself came about. He had been sickened, like the majority of his countrymen and women by the wanton violence of the Black and Tans. In the aftermath of the Rising, he had discovered within himself a great sympathy for the Irish ideals that had led to the conflict. Like the majority of the population his loyalty towards Redmond's Home Rule Party had waned, and he had actually been very happy when Sinn Fein swept up power following the 1918 elections. The British had then rounded up and imprisoned men like de Valera and Arthur Griffiths, but their roundup proved ineffective because it left the hardliners in control. Men like Michael Collins, Harry Boland and Cathal Brugha planned a vicious retaliation.

Working the ground in Dublin City had also opened his eyes to what was happening throughout the country. He knew, and understood, the fear generated by the Tans. Because they were closely associated with the Tans he could understand, but couldn't condone, the targeting and killings of members of the Royal Irish Constabulary (RIC). Recruitment for the RIC had fallen, and resignations followed hard on the heels of killings. The Irish people ostracized the RIC, refusing even to sit in the same church pew as an RIC member. Women who dated them had their hair shorn off. Anyone who fraternized with them was marked down for special treatment. But it was in Dublin that Troy witnessed the worst excesses of the Tans. Innocent folk were shot of hand - the Tans sometimes firing blindly, and at random, from the backs of trucks. He had held many funeral processions for such innocents.

Troy found himself sickened by the excesses of the Tans. He hated too the extent to which British censorship tried to worm its way in, and corrupt Irish social life. He found that cultural plays and songs were banned, and the streak of rebellion within his own soul cried out for redemption.

What finally turned Troy in favour of the rebels though hinged on the brutal and violent rape of Lucy Brown Corish. Like her husband Ben, and the Dublin journalist McAnthony he was outraged at the brutal assault on the young mother. His sermon from the pulpit the following Sunday reflected his new-found horror, and he told his parishioners he could understand people wanting to strike back. He was surprised by the sudden burst of applause that broke out at his words. He wasn't surprised when he was summoned to Tuite's residence to explain his actions.

THE CLOAK WAS A SOMEWHAT shadowy figure.

A detective working in the heart of the British establishment in Dublin - The Castle - the Cloak also had genuine Irish loyalties and regularly passed information to Collins. They had arranged to meet at one of their favourite hangouts - Vaughan's Hotel.

The Cloak eyed Collins over his cup of coffee and beneath his wide brimmed hat pulled low over his forehead. The man was wearing a dark suit. When he spoke his Dublin twang was very noticeable, and his pale green eyes were hooded.

"He won't be easy to take."

"Why's that?" Collins was intrigued.

"He always changes his routine. Regularly. Like clockwork. He's smart, intelligent. Uses disguises a lot, changes his appearance."

Michael Collins was having a discussion with one of his spies from the Castle - a police detective who supported the Irish cause. The cause of their discussion centred on the dangerous intelligence officer - Harry Sword. Collins had discovered that Sword was setting traps for him all over the city, and in one or two cases, the Cork man had only narrowed avoided capture. He had decided that Sword's continuing presence constituted a threat to his well-being, and his only option seemed to be to have his 'squad' take care of the Englishman.

However Sword was proving elusive.

He had learned lessons from the deaths of other Castle men. He trusted none of them as to his movements. He kept very much to himself.

"Does he have to be taken out?" the Cloak asked.

Collins looked at the man in surprise. He had never known the Cloak to show 'cold feet' before. He sipped his tea thoughtfully. Understanding dawned in his hazel eyes. "You like him, don't you?"

The Cloak shrugged. "Yeah, maybe I do. He's damned efficient. He's not without Irish sympathies either. He tried to stop some of the executions in '16."

"Oh, said Collins intrigued.

The cloak nodded seriously. "You'd like him too, if you met him."

"That's a pleasure I'll have to forego," Collins said grinning. "It might prove a little dangerous for my health."

"What if I could set up a meet?"

Collin's eyes narrowed. Did he really trust the Cloak? The man's help had been invaluable in the past...but still? What would be the purpose in meeting up with a British intelligence agent?

The Cloak sensed his doubt. The Dublin man smiled. "A matter of trust," he said cannily, smiling.

Collins was unapologetic. "I have to be cautious," he counselled. "The man's a British agent. What would be the point of meeting up with him?"

"A frank exchange of views perhaps. The man's mother was Irish."

Collin's cup froze on the way to his lips. He could catch on fast. He eyed his spy. "Do you think there's a chance...a chance he might turn?"

"Wouldn't have suggested it otherwise." The cloak waited expectantly.

He knew Collins. Knew the man wouldn't let this opportunity slip. He smiled when he saw the decision reached in the Cork man's eyes.

Collins put down his cup carefully and dabbed his mouth with a napkin. "Set it up," he ordered the Cloak. "I'll meet the man personally."

THE CLOAK MOVED IN mysterious circles. He must have known every pub in Dublin and quite a few beyond the Pale. He was often seen at race meetings, not to back the jee jees, but to pick up gossip from the who's who of society. Croke Park was another of his hangouts especially when there were good gaelic or hurling games scheduled; and as for the annual horse show in the RDS, well...that was a given. He had never missed it.

His list of contacts was legendary and there was nothing in Irish society that he didn't have some kind of a handle on. Perhaps that was what made him such a good detective.

MICHAEL COLLINS WAS nothing if not daring.

He took a seat opposite the blind man on the tram. Travelling around as a blind man often allowed Sword to see what he shouldn't have. Collins grinned into his face, giving the British intelligence agent the uncanny feeling that his ruse had been seen through. What the heck was that man grinning about?

Sword was dressed for the part - a long white frock-like coat, thin dark glasses that concealed his eyes, and a blind man's stick.

Collins admired the disguise.

"What are you grinning at, young man?" Sword tapped his cane impatiently.

"How do you know I'm grinning?" Collins countered.

"I can sense it."

"You're Harry Sword...the British Intelligence agent."

Sword was startled. "Who the blazes are you?" he quipped.

"The man you've been looking for."

"Collins?"

"That's right."

To give Sword his due, he didn't overreact. He gave an edgy glance to the side and rear, wondering if Collins was alone. The 'squad' had dragged a man off the trams before, a banker by the name of Bell who had been investigating the money links between the banks and Sinn Fein, and had shot him dead. Sword was wondering if he was about to share the same fate.

"I'm alone," Collins assured him, guessing the thoughts running through the head of the agent.

"What do you want?"

"A little talk...nothing more?"

The boldness of the Irish rebel was amazing. Sword concealed a grin of admiration. He admired guts. He thought rapidly. If Collins had wanted him dead, he wouldn't have played it like this. The 'squad' would simply have boarded and pumped a couple of shots into him. He wouldn't have known anything about it. He reached a quick decision. "I know a little café just off Sackville Street," he suggested.

"Perfect."

They remained seated for another two stops, and then both stood together. Collins took Sword by the arm as he tapped and limped his way forward. "Allow me to help you, sir?"

"Very kind of you, young man," said Sword, again wondering if this was a 'hit'. But the stop had been his suggestion. Nobody else stood to get off.

"THEY TELL ME YOUR MOTHER was Irish?"

"That's right," Sword confirmed. "A Cabra woman."

"A Dublin lass," Collins said, with obvious mirth. "How did you end up working against your own people?" The two men had taken a quiet booth having ordered a pot of tea for two. The tea was served with dried biscuits.

Sword sipped his tea, and munched thoughtfully on a biscuit. He'd always thought of his work as working for the Irish. True, he was army intel'. But he had often felt an affinity with Ireland and that was why he had chosen to live here. "Never quite thought of it like that," he remarked.

"Do you enjoy your work?"

"It has its moments."

"Could you see yourself ever switching allegiances?"

"No. Could you?"

Who was trying to turn whom? Collins wondered, annoyed and exasperated that his Castle spy was wrong. Sword seemed to be the dedicated Englishman. How could the Cloak have been so wrong in his assessment? Collins shifted uneasily. Was this a trap, set up for him? The Castle was offering 10,000 pounds for his head. A princely sum, and a tempting one in certain quarters.

Sword eyed the Irish rebel from behind his dark glasses. He memorized the man's features, the business-like look, the pin-striped suit. No wonder the rebel had been able to avoid capture for so long. A picture of him had appeared in the police rag Hue and Cry, but it hadn't been a good likeness.

Collins eyed him grimly. "You know you're on the wrong side, don't you?"

"How do you mean?"

"We're going to win." The words were delivered in a flat, emphatic tone with no hint of braggadocio, just a cast-iron certainty that things would turn out the way he had prophesied. The confidence of the Cork rebel was staggering.

Sword frowned. "You are going to...win?" he emphasised, drawing out the final word. Was it possible, Sword wondered inwardly. The belief of the man in front of him was infectious. The thought was mind-boggling. That the British Empire would fold and cave into Irish demands. Would London back down? He realised with a sudden start that it was possible - hadn't London already put a form of Home Rule on the table.

Collins was smiling at him. "You'd better believe we are going to win. We're going to take back our state. You've seen our support here...that's multiplied by our people in the States, in Australia, in Paris and elsewhere in Europe. We've gone too far to back down. Can you not see that?"

But all of a sudden he could see it. Sword knew with a sudden intuitive feeling that the Cork rebel was right. Irish freedom would be won. Where did that leave him? Out in the cold. A puppet on a string that had backed the wrong play and danced to the wrong tune. He needed time...time to think. Collins could be mighty persuasive, he realised. "And if I don't string along?" he asked.

Collins spread his hands placating. "That's your choice. You're a smart man...go with what your conscience tells you. You can throw in with us and reap the rewards. The offer's on the table. Throwing in with us is not risk free...there's still tough decisions ahead. You might want to consider it?"

Sword was silent. Collins was right on at least one point. Throwing his lot in the rebels was as risky as hell...if caught it would be certain he would face the gallows. Treason was a capital offence.

Collins eyed him shrewdly. He knew the thoughts milling about in the head of the intelligence agent. It was no easy step. He liked the cautious approach of Sword.

"You'll have a think about it?"

"I will," Sword said reflectively, tapping his cane against the floor in a nervous gesture.

"HOW DID IT GO?" THE Cloak asked curiously.

Nearly a week had gone by, a week in which Collins had heard no word back. It was obvious though that Sword had backed off in his pursuit and there had been no new attempts made at his apprehension. Collins considered the Cloak's question and remarked pensively: "I've heard nothing back...not yet?"

"He's obviously cautious," the Cloak said. "He's risking a lot."

Collins nodded thoughtfully. He said nothing to the Cloak about his plans. If Sword didn't make contact within the next week, then he had initiated plans to take care of the matter. He had identified a weak spot in Sword's routine - a favourite coffee shop. He hoped the man would make contact. The man's access to the Castle files were better than the Cloaks, and he would need the best intelligence he could gather if he was to beat the British at their own game.

The telephone suddenly rang. Sword's voice was muffled. "I'm in," he confirmed.

Collins winked at the Cloak. "It won't be no picnic, Harry?" he warned. Michael Collins was testing the man, searching his voice for any hint of indecision; any hint that he hadn't given the matter enough thought.

"I'm in, Michael." No hesitation, no doubt. The decision had been made.

"You won't regret it, Harry." Collins was delighted. He could scrap his plans to mount an attack on
the coffee shop, his men spared for other more important duties. Collins arranged to meet the man
again and put down the telephone. The Cloak
looked curious.

"Was that the man?"

"He's in," Collins enthused.

"What now then?"

"He'll be our 'eyes' and our 'ears' within the Castle. His information will act as a supplement to
yours. If there's any deviation in the reports, we'll
know he hasn't turned...and he can then be taken
care of. I know a way he can be taken...however, I really believe he's thrown in with us."

"He's not a devious type," the Cloak commented.
"If he hadn't wanted in he'd have told you out
straight. He's that type."

"I've no doubt you're right," Collins said, "but we
shouldn't forget he is...was British intelligence. He'll

have to be tested. It's best never to underestimate the auld enemy!"

SWORD WONDERED FOR the millionth time had he done the right thing.

Betrayal didn't come easy to a man like him. From the moment he had accepted Collin's offer, he knew he was leading a double life. One thing that kept him to his promise though was not the fact that he was betraying comrades he had once worked with, but the fact that many of those now working in the Castle were new men. Men brought in from the North and from England.

Sword didn't like this new breed.

He found them arrogant and crass. In a way the policies of Belfast and London hardened his new-found attitude, and he revelled in his new daring role. In many ways he was a man who liked living on the edge.

Whether that came from his fiery Irish mother he had never much thought about. It was however one of the things, which had attracted him to the kind of life that he led. He was intelligent enough to recognise that things were changing.

But in a place where suspicion was rife, Sword's changing shifts hadn't gone completely unnoticed. He was now under suspicion.

CHAPTER 11

TONY FELT A SHOCK COURSE through his veins as the knocking on his door intensified.

He sensed it wasn't good news. It was four in the morning. He could hear the distinctive sound of morning birds as his eyes stirred. Nature's alarm clock.

Reluctantly he swung his legs out of bed, and donned a dressing gown over his pyjamas.

He was surprised to see the apprentice on his doorstep, and realized with a shock that the youngster was crying. Frank Hennessy worked in the printing presses, and his thin hands were stained with dark ink. He brought the youngster into his kitchen and looked at the tears etched on the boy's face.

"Frank. What's wrong?" A nervous tic had started on Tony's brow.

"Conor's dead."

"Dead?"

The youngster looked at Tony in sympathy. He knew they had been friends. "His...his heart gave out. He died at midnight."

Tony blanched.

Conor Sweeney had been like a father to him. He felt the loss immediately. What was it Conor had said to him?

"Be the best you can be, Tony. Follow your heart...your dreams."

He felt the death of Sweeney would be a catharsis in his life. Things would now change. He sensed that.

The new year had brought changes that weren't welcome.

CONOR SWEENEY'S FUNERAL took place in Mount Argus.

The church was packed, and the mournful sound of bagpipes filled the crowded pews as the eulogy ended. McAnthony smiled in fond remembrance as he envisaged the colourful and purple prose Sweeney would have put on this gathering if had been around to see it.

Mary Sweeney was inconsolable. The light of her life was gone, and her steps were faltering as she followed the coffin from the church. Conor's sons carried their father from the church, manfully perched on their shoulders, their arms interlinked to support the weight. A request was put to Tony to help shoulder the weight and he agreed with alacrity.

"It would be an honour," he said, in a quiet, subdued tone to Conal - Conor's eldest son.

Conal smiled for the first time that day. "You know, my father always liked you. He said you were like a son, a brother."

"We all loved him, Conal."

Conal sniffed. "He was special, wasn't he?"

It was Tony's turn to smile. "You'd better believe it, kid."

THE CHANGES INITIATED by the new editorial team at the Irish Times offices in D'Olier Street following Conor Sweeney's death were just too much for McAnthony to swallow. The editorial line was just too pro-British for his liking, it ignored or chose to ignore the new nationalistic fervour that had built up in the country since the Rising, it was anti-Sinn Fein and anti-Irish, and to Tony's eyes it lacked the balance that Sweeney had tried to promote and encourage.

The new editor was Arthur Finn, a pompous balloon of a man with sagging skin, a double-jowled chin, and cold cloudy eyes as grey as a windswept stormy Aran day, who Tony had always detested. His thick lips curled in distaste as he read McAnthony's latest copy and summoned him to his office and flung his copy on to his mahogany desk. "What kind of rubbish is this?" he growled hoarsely. The room was filled with dark Cuban cigar smoke which Finn relished.

"What do you mean, Artie?" McAnthony piped up innocently. The article was a two thousand word piece on the women's movement - Inghidne na hEireann. Tony had filed the copy close to the deadline.

Finn's stubby tobacco stained fingers thumbed his copy. "Have you anything else?" he queried. "I'm not running this type of nonsense in my newspaper."

"You're not?" McAnthony was struggling to keep his temper in check. "Conor gave the go-ahead for the piece. He was thinking of covering the various women movements that had a nationalistic outlook...he was trying to give balance to our reporting.

Finn coughed harshly. "Sweeney's dead, McAnthony. There's a new team in town. The sooner you get your head around that fact the better off we'll all be. I want you to scrap this piece. Deliver new copy, and remember we want pro-British articles at this publication. Remember who our advertisers are. Are you reading me?"

"Loud and clear, Artie." So it had come down to this, McAnthony thought sourly.

He made no move to leave the office.

Finn's heavy eyebrows rose as McAnthony remained seated. "The deadline is closing in," he pointed out. In other words get the hell out of my office.

A hard decision formed in Tony's eyes. It was something he had been contemplating since the death of Conor. His level stare towards Finn made the man shift uncomfortably. "So you're not going to run with the piece?" Tony's words were delivered softly, with no hint of what was to follow.

"I've said all I'm going to say on the matter," Finn warned.

Tony stood up and gathered his article together. He reached to his inside pocket and withdrew an envelope he handed to Finn.

"What's this?"

"That's my resignation."

"Your...resignation?" Finn remained as still as a pole. "Look, let's not be hasty," he began.

McAnthony was walking towards the door. Finn got panicky. Though Editor-in-Chief at the Times since the death of Conor, he was answerable to a Board of Governors. They wouldn't be happy that one of their top political reporters had walked out. The man had incredible sources. McAnthony's hand was on the door knob when Finn croaked: "Walk out that door now, and I'll see to it that you never get a newspaper job in this town again."

Tony paused and swivelling on his heel he smiled coldly at Finn. "That's where you are wrong, Artie. I've already landed a job...you can't see it...you're too blind from where you're sitting...but there are changes afoot in this country. Big changes.

Momentous changes. You can take your pro-British slant and shove it where the sun don't shine...because I'm now warning you. If you don't change with the times, then this newspaper is finished. You think you'll still be seated in that chair a few years from now? Do you? The big difference between you and Conor is that he had the good sense to recognise how things were going...but you? You're totally blind...you can't see beyond your nose. Think about it. It's not called The Irish Times for nothing. You can sit in your ivory tower and wear your rose tinted glasses and Union Jack badges, and pretend nothing is happening in this country of ours, but one day you'll turn around and you'll find the country has bitten back. Your circulation figures will fall...your readers will disappear. Your advertisers won't want to know you. Do you think the Board will leave you in that seat then?"

"Are you finished?" Finn's voice was cold. Outrage masked his eyes, but a deep fear lurked there too, a fear that the harsh reality of McAnthony's prophecy might indeed come true. If McAnthony thought such a scenario likely then the chances of it happening it were high. Political matters were his forte.

"Mark my words, Artie," McAnthony warned, turning the door knob, and walking out. He didn't look back.

He had just opened a new door in his life. He hadn't lied to Finn. Arthur Griffith's had offered him work with the radical press...it was a step down, but he had other ways to supplement his income. A Boston weekly, well respected had contacted him to supply copy on hot Irish affairs for its Irish readership. He had never overlooked a challenge. He would deliver.

THE AMERICAN INFLUENCE on Irish affairs.

Irish Americans, many of whom had emigrated during the Famine years, had consolidated their positions in the land of plenty. They were a powerful lobby group, and they had attached themselves to all areas of society. Some were in traditional roles - the New York City Police Department and the New York Fire Department. Others had gone a step further and had immersed themselves in American politics, but always with one eye open on the country they had left, and they used their new found influence and money to try and change things for the better in their home country.

The famine ships had delivered them to this new land, but their homeland would never be forgotten. It was carved in their hearts. The miles they had put between themselves and their beloved country were very real, but they hadn't forgotten what it meant to be Irish. They hadn't forgotten the auld enemy.

In places like New York and Boston Irish ghettoes sprang up. Ceilis and traditional music nights helped to foster the Irish spirit that still reigned deep in their hearts. The feeling burnt with a passion that would never die. It was unquenchable. Ablaze.

The better newspapers helped to keep them informed of what was happening back home. Irish newspapers also sprang up, run by Irish American editors and journalists. It was pressure from far-flung Irish havens like the Americas and Australia that had forced the British into stopping the executions of the rising leaders. It was American and Australian dollars that had helped fund the uprising - the money being used to purchase weapons outright or to curry political favours.

The American influence was something the British couldn't afford to ignore. They valued their American friends too highly. They also knew that America would be probably be drawn into the battle raging in Europe against the Kaiser. The outcome would then turn in Britain's favour.

In 1917, the sinking of the Lusitania twelve miles off the Cork coast finally brought the Americans into the First World War. The tide had turned against Germany and her allies.

McAnthony had written at length about the tragedy, both in the radical press at home and in the American newspapers. His engaging analysis won him many admirers, both at home and abroad. His cutting insights into the tragedy and the trigger effect on American public opinion were bang on the mark, and nobody was very surprised when America finally declared war on Germany. His rising journalistic profile didn't go down unnoticed with his former employers, who by now were beginning to sense the sweeping change coming over Europe as a whole.

A board meeting was called and changes were announced.

Summoned with no fanfare to the meeting, Finn was told in no uncertain terms that the Irish Times had to change with the times or die. Foolishly he protested. Nothing was done there and then, but the board was marking its time - Finn would have to go.

TROY HAD HEARD SOMETHING trouble-
some in the confessional, and his conscience was
bothering him.

An altar boy had come to him in the confessional and had stated, somewhat fearfully, that Father
Tom McGinley, Troy's supervisor, had been forcing
himself on the youngster in a sexual way. Troy was
deeply shocked and he questioned the boy further,
perhaps more sharply than he had intended. The boy
was adamant and Troy who knew the lad from Sunday services found himself believing the lad.

He wondered what he could say that could heal
the lad, and then he realised that nothing he could
say would help. For the first time in his priestly life
he was at a loss for words.

The silence grew in the confessional.

Troy started, realizing the boy had asked him
something. "Huh?" he grunted.

"Penance, Father," the boy was saying. "What's
my penance?"

"No penance," Troy replied.

"Huh?" It was the boy's turn to be confused. Realising this, Troy changed tack. "Okay, lad. One Hail Mary."

"Just one, Father?"

"Yes, lad," Troy confirmed, his mind racing. What could he do about this? Go to Tuite? A scowl hit his features as he realised he was in a confessional. Confessions were sacrosanct; the details not to be discussed. He realised the boy was leaving.

"Hang on, lad," Troy burst out. "These allegations are very serious. I'm going to need time to look into all this. Your real penance is to stay away from McGinley."

"But what about Sundays, Father?"

"Never mind your duties there, lad. I'll explain to McGinley that you're sick or something. Leave that man to me. I'll sort it."

Troy was angry. He thought of what he knew about the older priest. The man had welcomed him to the parish when he first started, but there had been something about him that made Troy keep his distance. McGinley had three cronies, all priests of his own age but Troy had noticed how they would clam up if he, or any of the other young priests, approached. He knew they were called the Four Horsemen of the Apocalypse because they often went riding together, but Troy was now wondering if it was just horses they were riding. He felt betrayed and he felt that McGinley had betrayed the ethos of the entire priesthood. He also felt sickened.

He dismissed the lad with a promise to look into the whole sordid manner. He decided to confront McGinley.

McGinley smiled at him as he approached, but the smile slid from his ruddy features at Troy's cold expression and opening words. "What's your game, McGinley?"

"Game?"

"With the altar boys?"

McGinley flushed, and Troy saw the guilt in the Donegal man's eyes. "Altar boys?"

"Don't play games with me, Father?" Troy said. "You'll leave those lads alone in the future or so help me."

"You'll what?" McGinley was sneering.

Troy lashed out, sinking his fist deep into the stomach of the older priest and leaving him retching on the floor. Troy's voice was very quiet when he spoke again. "You'll leave them alone or I'll kill you."

The words were delivered in a quiet, even tone, instantly believable, instantly credible. McGinley looked at Troy and said nothing. Wisely.

Troy said nothing else. He stormed off and didn't bother chiding himself with the fact that he had threatened to kill another human being. Sure, hadn't Moses resorted to that.

CHAPTER
12

THE COUNTRY WAS GALVANISED.

Feelings had polarized since the shootings of the Rising leaders. The inevitable victim was the Home Rule party. In the elections of '18 the party was suddenly decimated.

The country had radically altered in favour of Sinn Fein. Irish people like McAnthony and O'Sullivan who had campaigned relentlessly for just such an outcome felt justified and morally charged as the results came in.

Christmas was just around the corner, and Tony had a surprise for Angela, which he was about to spring on St Stephen's Day. He had decided to ask her to be his wife.

He had already bought the engagement ring in a jewellery shop on Grafton Street. He hoped she would say yes.

Change was everywhere that Christmas.

Since the death of Conor Sweeney, Tony had felt an estrangement with the Irish Times. His resignation followed soon after.

He was now working for Arthur Griffith and the radical press. His writings were more political, antagonistic. The Rising had had an effect on Tony and had affected his views in a number of ways.

THINGS HAD NOT BEEN easy for Minnie in the last two years.

The elections of 1918 held no interest for her, and her general apathy and bitterness meant she didn't vote. Money problems meant she had to go out and find work herself. She found work packing biscuits for Jacobs.

Since the loss of her husband and eldest son at the Somme life had proved more difficult for the McGuire family. She received a paltry pension from the British government for her loss, but it wasn't enough to live on. Her other sons had become somewhat unmanageable, without the steadying influence of her husband, and ran about like vagabonds through the streets of Dublin - pilfering and stealing. She also suspected one or two were smoking.

Officers from the Dublin Metropolitan Police - the Peelers - had been to her door several times in the past two years, and she had made innumerable visits to the courts.

One of her daughters was pregnant. Another worry.

SEVERAL WEEKS WENT by.

The wedding was getting closer. Lucy went shopping with Angela looking for that perfect wedding dress.

Dublin was undergoing change at last. The Rising was now over a year ago. The rebuilding had been slow. Rubble lay strewn for months. Some businesses remained closed for good, which didn't help the corporation with its rates and caused inner city unemployment.

With rebuilding in full swing, men like Billy Hannafin found plenty of employment. His rebel sons had also joined him in the building game, Dec becoming a carpenter like himself and Ciaran going down the brickie route. Both pulled in good money. Neither had fully abandoned their rebellious streak.

It was a side to them that Billy intended keeping close tabs on. He could only do so much though. Both were now dating and would probably flee the family nest as soon as they had gathered the necessary shillings. They were now young men, and since they were earning money, could, and often did, make their own decisions.

In Europe, the war which had engulfed the whole world was finally over, but not without a huge cost in human suffering and death. A new killer had emerged, perhaps even more frightening than war; a deadly strain of H1N1 influenza. People were frightened anew because they knew they were no more immune than the person next to them.

TONY HAD DECIDED TO follow an age old Irish tradition in asking Angela for her hand. He decided to ask her on Saint Stephen's day, after the customary festivities had died down a bit. He put it to Jonjo first as he believed in traditionalism, and he wanted the old man's blessing.

Jonjo poured him a glass of whiskey, and took time to fill up his pipe before answering him. "Do you love her?" he asked, lighting up his pipe and blowing the smoke contentedly towards the low cottage ceiling. The room wasn't a big one, but it was comfortable and warm. Briquettes of peat burned in the hearth, and there was a smell of toast as bread slowly browned on special pits near the fire. The house was empty except for Jonjo and Tony. Angela had gone out with her brothers to work the cobwebs out after the Christmas Day dinner by taking a long stroll out by the sand dunes and the Atlantic. She had seemed surprised when Tony hadn't joined them, but he had feigned an illness, and he encouraged her to go when she decided to stay with him. In the end she had gone, not liking to be the one to break with family traditions.

"Yes, Jonjo," he replied. "I do love her. I've loved her virtually since the day we met. I'm head over heels in love with your daughter and I don't want to go through this life without her by my side." He watched Jonjo lifting the toast off the cooking spits and buttering them with thick slices of butter that was made on the farm. He accepted a slice from the old man, and took another sip of his whiskey. A

Christmas tree was nicely decorated in the corner of the room, almost reaching to the thick oak beams that straddled the ceiling.

Jonjo took another pull at his pipe. "Marriage ain't all plain sailin'," he pointed out, using his pipe to emphasise his words. "It can be damned tricky at times, but if you're willing to work hard at it, I don't see any reason why it shouldn't work out for the pair of ye."

It took Tony a moment to digest the old man's words. "Halleluia," he shouted, a huge smile breaking out on his face, making him look for a moment like a gangly sixteen year old. He held out his hand to the old man. "Thanks, Jonjo. You won't regret it. I'll take good care of her for you."

"I know you will, my boy," he acknowledged, smiling back. "When will you ask her?"

"Tomorrow."

He nodded solemnly.

Christmas 1918 proved a happy one for Tony and Angela.

Angela had accepted his marriage proposal. He had taken her for a walk along the beach at Fenit, and he had popped the question. The crash of white-frothed waves behind them along the desolate coast-line had nearly drowned out her reply. The white horses were making their presence felt. There was no mistaking the joy on her face however.

She came into his arms, and their cold lips met. "Yes," she mouthed, knowing he hadn't heard her re-ply. "Yes...yes...yes!"

The chill wind of the sea flooding in from the Atlantic was forgotten as they held one another close. He slipped the engagement ring on to her fin-ger, and a smile played around her lips.

"I'm no longer cold," she shouted into his ear.

"Neither am I," he shouted back.

They moved together up the beach, their arms around one another united with joy every step of the way. Their love for another was as sure as the coloured pebbles beneath their feet as they strolled along the deserted beach. The pebbles crunched, like the shifting sands, like the shifting tide of Irish history.

THE WEDDING WAS A BIG affair.

Folk being something thrifty at the time and careful with the shillings, Angela decided to wed using her late mother's wedding dress, which had been kept specially packed in tissue paper and a dry box for just such an occasion. The men all wore tophats and suits, the shirts all pinned with dickiebows and ties.

A guard of honour was formed by the women of Cumann na mBan outside the small church. The church itself was built of stone and looked like it had stood the test of time over hundreds of years.

Tony was nervous as he awaited his bride at the church, but when the nuptials were all over, he announced it as the best day of his life.

When Angela arrived, she was beautiful and he told her so. She had something funny in her hand

and she laughed when she saw his quizzical expression. "It brings good luck," she explained to him. "It's
a horseshoe."

He still looked baffled.

She smiled demurely. "It's a country thing."

Their brief conversation happened after Jonjo
had led his daughter up the aisle, and shook hands
briefly with Tony, but came to an end as the priest
appeared. However, he was smiling as he launched
the service.

The reception was held in a dance hall nearby.
The band was made up of locals, young men and
women who could bang out tunes on the bodhran,
the accordion, and the tin whistle.

Following the meal and the speeches, Tony
asked his new bride for a dance.

Angela smiled and said: "You'll have to make
sure my feet stay on the floor."

"Why's that?"

"So the faeries don't snatch me off."

He laughed. "What?"

Her expression was so serious that he laughed harder.

"It's not funny, Tony," she warned.

His laughter died. "You don't really believe that hogwash, do you?"

She didn't say anything.

Smiling at her new husband, Angela thought to herself that it was also her best day.

What could go wrong?

Everything, as it happened.

CHAPTER 13

TONY FOUND HIMSELF approving of Collin's new strategy.

He recognised that Collins intelligence must be good, and suspected he had key informers in the Castle.

Collins was making it difficult for the 'G' men to operate.

The squad Collins had assembled were merciless and ruthless. They hunted down Castle spies and assassinated key targets. The Dog Smith, a notorious 'G' man had succumbed to the squad's fatal charms.

Working with Arthur Griffiths had given McAnthony a unique insight into the thinking behind these new tactics. He could sense that the British didn't like this new type of fighting.

The War of Independence was about to take a turn for the worse. The British had decided to play dirty too.

Convicts had been released from English prisons and pressed into military service. These were no ordinary soldiers though. In England they had been in prison for murder, rape and other serious crimes. The Black and Tans were about to be unleashed on an unsuspecting Irish public.

Within months the War of Independence had become known by another name - The Tan War.

A series of events were about to be unleashed by the arrival of the Tans. Everyone was frightened of the Tans - they soon developed a reputation for cold-blooded killing. They fired indiscriminately from the backs of lorries. They separated young sons from their mothers and shot them out of hand. One mother had found her two sons propped dead against a wall, with biscuit tins on their heads.

The Tans engendered fear everywhere they went.

Since arriving in Ireland they had sacked and burnt Balbriggan, Cork and Thurles. They had a hand in the murder of Thomas MacCurtain, the Mayor of Cork. Terence MacSwiney had died after a hunger strike to the death, and following hard on the heels of his death the British hanged Kevin Barry - the Republican cause had yielded further Irish patriots and martyrs.

Dublin wasn't the only place of IRA actions. In the country RIC men were gunned down. No quarter was given.

A shotgun poking through a hedge would blast the RIC man as he cycled by on his rounds. Often the RIC were accompanied by the Tans, and ambushes were often set to take out the whole party.

Tony himself had witnessed the unsavoury aspects of the Tans. He wrote critically of them in the radical press.

He had received overt threats, but Tony had powerful, dangerous friends. Though the pen was a mighty sword, some who had threatened him found themselves floating face downwards in the dark waters of the Liffey. The rebels took no prisoners. They looked out for their own. Since Tony's stand in the GPO alongside the rebels, he was recognised as a dangerous man in his own way.

He commanded respect.

Men knew about him. They knew he'd been locked up after the Rising. They knew he had paid a price. They knew they could trust him. They knew he could keep his mouth shut.

Even Michael Collins had recognised a latent power in the journalist. "Give that man a gun," he'd often jest. "And we'd have one hell of a rebel."

The Tan War was about to get very personal for Tony McAnthony.

The Tans were active countrywide, but lately they had been carrying out a lot of operations in the rebel county - Cork.

Angela was worried about her father and brothers. And then came the news they dreaded. Henry O'Sullivan had been gunned down.

The facts were sketchy, but one thing became quickly apparent. He had been gunned down in cold blood.

Angela was inconsolable.

"Poor Boxer," she sobbed. "Why him? He wouldn't have hurt a fly."

"There's no rhyme or reason why, luv," Tony said, trying to find the right words to comfort her. He felt the loss keenly himself. Henry had been like a brother. His arm was around her shoulders, her head was buried in his chest. "These Tans...they're just scum. Murderers."

"What will Jonjo do around the farm with Henry gone?" Angela was distraught. "He relied on Boxer more than any other man to run the place," she wailed. "How's he going to cope?"

"Don't worry about it, luv. We'll figure something out. We can help and perhaps one of the brothers? Perhaps Tadhg?

Angela shook herself together. "I'll get ready," she said. Kerry was a five year train journey away.

When she returned she was wearing mourning colours - black.

He bit his lip. He could tell she had been crying. His heart went out to her. He didn't know what to say for the best. In the end he said nothing. He was there for her. That was what really mattered.

She was numb with grief. Her face was composed in that tight, stoical expression people assume when death comes knocking at the door. She gave him a weak smile. "Ready?" she muttered.

"You don't want me to take the car?"

"No. The train is faster."

Which was true. The steam trains could really move.

Henry's death had shaken Jonjo.

Everyone could see that. The neighbours rallied around, helping with the farm work. Jonjo himself rose early to milk the cattle, hoping that perhaps the work would lift his mood and make him forget the tragic loss.

The man seemed to have aged a lifetime. He'd seen death before, of course, with his wife and some of his clan. Though shaken by this latest tragedy he remained stoically upright in his bearing. His faith was staggering, a belief in a Higher Power.

The wake had been a curiously sober affair and had taken place in the farmhouse. Neighbours gathered from far and near.

Henry was laid out in his best Sunday suit, his face oddly composed in the coffin. His old boxing gloves had been placed on his cold hands and a crucifix he had worn in the ring lay on his chest.

In the kitchen folk gathered to talk. To reminisce about old times. They told funny stories about the deceased, chuckling quietly among themselves.

Remembering happier times. It was a real Irish wake. The drink and the sandwiches flowed.

"Remember the time," one man recounted, chuckling and bringing tears and laughter to his listeners, "how the Boxer fought Dingle McGee to a standstill."

Even Dingle couldn't repress a laugh at that one.

"Recall another time he was trying to get the horses in from the upper meadows," another man recounted. "Think they'd come. You know how the Boxer loved the horses. He had to take a stick to them in the end."

They laughed again, imagining the scene.

THE SEVEN MAN SQUAD had studied the layout of the barracks intensely.

Many of them had known Boxer O'Sullivan, and one of the men had even fought with him in the ring. This man had a permanently crooked nose as a result of the Boxer's right hook, but he had still volunteered for this dangerous mission to avenge his friend. The Volunteers belonged to a man to one of the toughest Kerry Brigades, and they were all heavily armed.

All wanted to meet up with the sergeant who had so brutally put out the Boxer's lights. They wondered how he would stack up when the odds were no longer in his favour. More details had come to light since that fateful morning.

It had been rumoured that the sergeant had always been a bitter enemy of Jonjo. He had hated his son's prowess in the ring. He had once lost a sizeable amount of money on one of Henry's challengers, and he had never forgiven the Kerry fighter for this. With the backing of the tans, the sergeant, who went by the name of Hayden, but whom everyone knew as the Turk because of his swarthy florid features, had baited the young Kerryman with taunts about a local sweetheart. The Boxer had tried to retaliate in his usual manner, with a swift right upper hook. But the Turk had stepped back out of reach, laughing at his foe. He had drawn his revolver with nonchalant ease and had gunned the young Kerryman down in cold blood.

The barracks had a thatched roof and two of the volunteers immediately set it alight. Half blinded by smoke and sleep the RIC men came unwittingly out into the open, and were rounded up by the remaining volunteers.

Dingle McGee, the hardbitten volunteer who had once fought Henry in the ring stepped closer to the captured men. His voice when he spoke was harsh, unrelenting. "Where's the Turk?" he demanded.

The men were silent.

"I'll count to three," Dingle warned, "then I'm opening fire." He cocked the heavy revolver.

An RIC man gulped, and pointed towards the back of the burning building. "He escaped out the back."

"Alone?"

"Yeah."

Dingle turned to his men. He picked out the toughest and smartest. "Let's go find him," he ordered.

Within moments two of his men brought a shaking Turk to the crouched figure of McGee. "We found him hiding in some bushes," one of the men mocked.

Dingle looked at the captured RIC man with scorn. "Hayden," he said quietly, "I understand you like gunning down unarmed men."

"Henry?"

Dingle nodded.

"It was a mistake," the Turk announced, as though his words could alter matters.

Dingle nodded again. "A bad mistake," he agreed. "You might want to say an act of contrition."

Hayden blanched. "And then what?"

"Then I'm going to shoot you."

"Look," the Turk began to plead.

"Say your prayers, sergeant."

But the Turk was beyond praying. His panic stricken eyes swept left, swept right, seeking a way out of this.

Dingle cocked his gun again and fired. The Turk slid noiselessly to the ground, dead before he hit it.

"What will we do with these?" one of the younger members said, pointing at the quaking figures huddled in front of the building.

Dingle spoke from the corner of his mouth. "Let them go." He looked them over with cold eyes. "We took the Turk out...you men know why we did that. Some of you may also have been involved. I'm giving you notice now. Any more killings of that sort around here won't be tolerated. You men all have families. Go home to them. Think about your country. Quit persecuting your own folk. Any man that has an argument with that knows where to find me...but if you want to end up like Hayden out back, just say so."

There were no takers.

The volunteers stripped the men of weapons and retreated back into the night.

CHAPTER
14

MINNIE HAD BECOME ESTRANGED from her neighbours.

Her daughter Maggie had given birth to a baby boy. It was yet another mouth to feed.

She had met a new man, who helped in bringing more money into the house, but it was the Queen's shilling. The new man in her life was hated in the vicinity, not because he was English, but because he was one of those hated 'Tans'.

Minnie didn't care what her neighbours thought.

She had mouths to feed.

She didn't really notice the visits of her friends drying up, and she ignored their warnings about her new man. His name was Hugh Stewart, and he possessed a hulking violent presence in Minnie's home.

Behind her back he gloated to his friends in barracks about the bit of Irish ass he had every night.

In the neighbourhood he was feared.

He kept Minnie's children in line, often by giving the lads a belt around the ear, and usually when she wasn't around.

He had a hold on Minnie that was frightening to see, but Minnie was no spring chicken anymore, and the years of childbirths were catching rapidly up.

Hugh was often drunk.

His language was like his appearance - unkempt. He had shaggy hair which would never have been tolerated in the regular forces of the Crown.

They called him Shaggy in the tenements, but never to his face.

He sat now in Minnie's sitting room, watching her knit a sweater, whilst drinking a bottle of Guinness.

"Waste of time," he muttered, darkly.

"What is?" Minnie's tone was patient.

"K...knitting," he slurred.

Minnie eyed him over her glasses, but continued her work. "It keeps me busy."

"Let's go to bed," he suggested.

She gave him a look. "Not now. I'm not in the mood. Besides you're drunk."

"I ain't drunk."

Minnie laughed. "You're as drunk as a skunk."

He stood up and slapped her. Her knitting hit the ground as she fingered her cut mouth in shock. He had never lifted a finger to her before.

Minnie was a tough Dublin character. She eyed this hulking presence in her home and launched herself at him, her hands clawing at his face and digging deep into his flesh.

He laughed and threw her off.

"Get out," she screamed at him.

Mercifully he went.

Shaggy was mumbling into his whisky bottle.

He still couldn't believe Minnie had attacked him. He fingered the welts along his face and mumbled: "I'll fucking show her who's boss later.

The boozer was about to shut.

Shaggy spotted Lucy leaving the pub on her own. He followed. Another piece of nice ass, he thought.

He caught up with her, and dragged her into a laneway. His senses dulled by drink, he tried kissing her, but she struggled away, her knee coming up into his groin.

Shaggy was so drunk he didn't feel the pain.

He clamped his hand over Lucy's mouth to drown her scream. His other hand reached down, ripping her clothes, moving between her legs.

Lucy fought hard, but she was no match for this hulking brute.

Shaggy forced himself into her, and left her for dead in the alleyway.

THE INCESSANT KNOCKING on his door startled Tony and reminded him of the night Conor had died. He climbed out of bed, threw on a robe, and went to answer the door. Ben Corish stood there, his face white.

"It's Lucy," he explained. "She's been taken to hospital."

"What's wrong?" said Angela, appearing on the stairs in her nightgown, a startled look on her face.

"Your friend Lucy," Tony said. "Ben said she's been taken to hospital. Come in, out of the cold, man. Before you catch your death."

They retreated into the kitchen, and Angela filled the kettle.

Ben dropped into a chair, his features haggard and flushed, his face remaining ashen.

"What's wrong with Lucy, Ben?" Angela's eyes reflected her concern.

"They found her in an alleyway near Moore Street. Unconscious, somebody really worked her over. And..."

"And?" Tony prompted.

"She had been raped."

"What?" blurted Angela, totally shocked.

"Raped," Ben repeated, wiping a tear from his eye.

Tony exchanged a glance with his wife, and saw the look of horror in her eyes. He moved quickly to her side. He put his arm around her. "Easy," he said to her. "Easy."

"Oh Ben, I'm so sorry. Who'd want to do such a thing?"

Ben shook his shoulders helplessly. "Don't know," he mumbled. "She went out to meet friends in a pub. It was something she did every Friday. The other traders, she liked their company on Friday nights."

Tony had learned one thing as a journalist.

Tenacity.

He was good at his job because he had an ability to dig for the truth, no matter how hard the obstacles that were thrust into his path. He also had a deep sensitivity, that surfaced now as he left the hospital, and went in search of the pub where Lucy had been drinking. He was angered by what happened to their friend.

Angela had volunteered to look after Lucy's children whilst Ben waited anxiously outside her ward. Tony was happy with that arrangement - it gave him time to do what he had to do.

The pub was an early morning one, and had just opened when he arrived. The barman eyed him.

"What will it be, mister."

"Put us on a pint."

"Coming up."

The barman filled the pint-glass three quarters of the way with creamy black stout and left it to settle on the counter. He eyed his customer. He hadn't seen him in here before. "Just off work?" he asked, conversationally.

Tony shook his head. "Just back from the hospital."

"Oh?" The barman looked curious.

Tony filled him on what had happened last night. The barman was shocked.

"She was drinking here?" he asked. "What was her name?"

"Lucy Brown Corish."

The barman shook his head, and finished off pulling the pint. A scowl had appeared on his forehead.

"What do I owe you?"

"On the house," he growled. He looked at his customer. "I wasn't on myself, last night," he explained. "So I wouldn't know who had been around. I know Lucy though - she drinks in here every Friday night with her friends."

"So I gather." Tony watched as the man removed his apron and snapped it onto the counter. He raised his eyebrow.

"Wait here," the barman ordered. "Jimmy was on last night. He's the manager. He's asleep upstairs. I'll go wake him."

When the manager appeared he looked dishevelled and tired. His voice was sharp as he addressed Tony. His shirt was hanging out over his trousers.

"This about Lucy?" he grunted.

"Did you hear what happened her?"

"No...what?"

"When she left here last night...she was followed, and raped."

"Raped?" Jimmy was suddenly wide-awake. He clapped his hand to his face, and rubbed ruefully at the stubble on his jaw. He eyed his barman and said: "Give this gent a drink on the house and pour me a scotch. A stiff one."

"Raped," Tony confirmed. "Somebody worked her over pretty good too. She's in the hospital."

"Jesus," said Jimmy. He swallowed a large measure of the scotch.

"Any idea who followed her out?"

Jimmy was still fingering his stubble. "That bastard," he suddenly ground out, his memory of the night before flooding back.

"Who?" There was a hint of violence in McAnthony's tones.

"A Tan."

"What's his name?"

"Shaggy. Everyone knows him as Shaggy. He's living with that McGuire woman. He drinks in here regularly."

"Where are they shacked up?"

"Gardiner Street."

Tony drained his Guinness. "Obliged for the drink," he said.

"What are you going to do, mister?"

Tony smiled coldly. "I wouldn't worry about it, but one thing..."

"Yes?"

"You won't be seeing him in here again."

"YOU WANT A WHAT?"

Michael Collins eyed the Dublin journalist in astonishment. McAnthony sighed heavily and told Collins about the attack on Lucy. The Cork man was silent when he had finished speaking. He decided a warning wouldn't be amiss. "It isn't easy shooting a man, Tony."

"I know."

"Why don't you let me take care of this animal for you...I've men in the 'squad' who would only be too happy to take care of this matter."

Tony shook his head. "This is personal," he stated.

Collins sighed. "Well, I'll lend you two men. You'll need help to take him. Do you know anything about guns?"

"I know which part is the business end," he said, smiling grimly.

Collins just looked at him. His silence spoke volumes.

Tony's grin faded. "Yeah, I know a little about them...I've fired a few before."

"Leave it with me for a day or two," Collins advised.

TROY LEFT HIS STATION at the pro-cathedral with a worried frown on his face.

A parishioner had come running to him with news of the attack on Lucy Brown Corish. He liked that young woman. He walked with a fast clipped angry pace towards the Mater Hospital.

Since the arrival of the Tans things were going from bad to worse in Ireland. He wondered would things ever get better?

BLOODY SUNDAY.

Troy said the eleven o'clock and began looking forward to the match in Croker later. He enjoyed an early roast beef dinner, and set out at about one. He was a big GAA fan. He had heard of the shootings early this morning throughout Dublin.

The word on the streets was that they were British agents from the Castle. He knew that could bring trouble.

Just how much trouble he would witness later that day.

THE 'SQUAD' HAD BEEN busy. They had been mobilized the night before.

The hand-picked men from London had been compromised. They mostly lived in the Dublin 2 and 4 areas of the city, and to their neighbours they were known as the 'Hush Hush' men. They had aroused suspicions soon after their arrival in Ireland, especially the way they went out at night in breach of the military curfews. It could only mean one thing -

they were military themselves. They were all marked men. The 'squad' now had their names and addresses. Guns and ammunition were checked and re-checked.

Had the London men have had the benefit of forward vision they would have been astounded at the breach of security in relation to their activities, and the fact that one by one they were marked down for a bullet. Irish style.

LUCY OPENED HER EYES.

She immediately wished she hadn't. Memories of the night before flooded her brain, and she turned her head sharply with a hiss of suppressed fury bursting from her lips. She felt sore everywhere.

She recognised her surroundings, recognising the fact she was lying in a hospital bed. The harsh antiseptic smell would have told her anyway.

Both Ben and Angela saw her movement and stirred. They were both tired. They had maintained a vigil all night beside her bed, wandering in and out of the ward at various times during the night, to replenish their own bodies with hot drinks. Angela was somewhat surprised that Tony hadn't returned yet.

He hadn't said where he was going.

Angela had a feeling though that he was following through his investigative side, and looking closer into the brutal attack last night.

TONY HAD LOST HIS VIRGINITY when he was nineteen, when in the first year of college he had befriended a 'Cailin deas', but he was thirty four when he lost his political virginity, or naivety, and it happened on the Sunday morning when he accompanied two of Michael Collins 'squad' men to Minnie McGuire's house in Gardiner Street. The street had mostly tenement style houses owned by the landlord class, who rented out the small hovels within to working class families. TB was a curse of these tenements, and sickness clung to the occupants with the obstinacy of the clothes hanging to dry over dilapidated balconies.

"Got a light, mac?"

The two republicans had been through this routine so often in the past that it had become second nature. Flint had asked the question, a cigarette dangling from his stubby fingers as he put the question to Shaggy, who had been under surveillance for the past two days. Flint and Farmer. Easy names to remember. Neither looked liked killers, which perhaps explained why they were so effective.

They had agreed the set-up with McAnthony. Neither man knew who he was. Collins hadn't bothered to explain that. Both assumed he must be a member of the IRB they hadn't run across before. They were also under strict orders that the fatal shot was McAnthony's sole responsibility, and that they were to assist only. Period!

Shaggy paused to give the man a light. He was in good humour. His mates had called to tell him to join them - they were on their way to Croke Park to shoot up the place.

"Ta," said Flint, his cold grey eyes flicking beyond the Black and Tan man. Tony moved the car up towards them.

Farmer moved in behind Shaggy. He stuck the business end of a pistol into Shaggy's ribs.

The Englishman's face registered shock. "Hey, what is this?"

"Shut up," Farmer ordered, "and move." Flint helped his sidekick to bundle the Black and Tan man into the back of the waiting car.

Tony sped off. He cut through a number of side streets, near Croke Park as a matter of fact, and turned down towards the Royal Canal. He brought the car to a stop near the back of Mountjoy Prison and took his pistol from the dash-board as Flint and Farmer bundled Shaggy out of the car and tossed him on the wasteground. The Englishman's eyes were wide with fear.

"Oh," he grunted. He eyed the gun in Tony's hand. "What are you going to do? Yeah?"

Tony didn't answer. He looked into the Black and Tan's eyes and said: "Lucy Brown Corish."

"Who?"

"The Horse and Hound."

"Listen..."

Tony aimed the gun between the Tan's eyes and pulled the trigger. The shot lifted the Tan man erect, cutting off his plea mid-flow, killing him instantly and sending his body flying back into the water.

Flint approached him. "Nice shot, mister," he said. "Give me the gun."

Tony handed the gun to the man. He turned away.

The current was beginning to drag at the Tan's body.

A fusillade of shots reached their ears. They strained their ears. Farmer looked pale. "What's going on? At Croker?"

Flint shrugged. "There's a match today, isn't there?"

"Yeah," Farmer agreed. "But what's all the shooting about?"

Flint didn't know and told him so. "We'd better get out of here," he said.

Tony heard the shooting, but the real shot he could hear was the one he had just fired. He felt ill. He didn't know what the shooting was about up in Croker either, but he agreed with Flint's assessment that they should get out of here.

NOBODY KNEW HOW IT started.

The Tans were out seeking blood. English blood had been shed that morning, and the Tans figured some of the killers may have gone to the game.

Nobody was expecting them to open up with machineguns on the crowd.

Croke Park, the home of GAA football and hurling, was immersed with blood. They said later that Hill 16 had been awash with blood. The Hill had the rep' of always holding the more hardline elements of the crowd, so it was perhaps inevitable that the tans concentrated their fire there.

TROY WAS SHAKING BY the time he got back to his home that evening.

He immediately poured himself a stiff brandy. His clothes were splattered with blood. He had said the last rites into the ears of many of the victims, but he still could not believe that the Tans had opened fire in the way that they had.

He had been shocked.

The news had reached him, of course, of the deaths of British intelligence agents in the early hours of the morning. The Cloak and Sword had provided excellent intelligence. The Squad had been galvanised by the information, and the special Dublin brigade set up by Collins, had carried out the executions to the letter.

But the British forces had reacted badly to this setback. Stunned into a response, their reply had been swift and bloody.

CHAPTER
15

ON BLOODY SUNDAY, TONY and Angela found some time together; weekday schedules were becoming busier for both and time spent together was becoming a luxury. Angela stroked his thigh. "You're very moody tonight," she observed. "What's bothering you? The killings in Croke Park today?"

He had debated telling her, but could not see the sense in upsetting her. She was uptight enough about her friend as it was. He lit a cigarette, his thoughts dark. The whole day had been somewhat surreal. The tension of the early morning had dissipated like the

285

smoke from the pistol shot which he had fired that afternoon, the casual banter of the two republicans had unsettled his state of mind, and though he hadn't expected to feel good about the killing of another human being, he knew that he had overstepped a certain boundary in his own mind. He questioned his judgement. Who was he to be jury, judge and executioner? Why had he taken it upon himself to act in such a callous manner? Lucy was Angela's friend. Sure. But what was she to him? A casual acquaintance? A friend? How had he got so involved in this mess? Angela was looking at him out of those big blue eyes.

"Well?"

He gave her a weak grin. "It's nothing...I'm just in bad form." He inhaled his cigarette deeply and blew a cloud of smoke towards the ceiling. He stubbed it and immediately lit up another.

"You just put one out?" she said.

"So?"

"You shouldn't be chain-smoking. They're bad for you."

"Christ woman," he snapped, "get off my back, will you?"

She withdrew from him, pumping her legs up beneath her body, her arms folded in against her body. Defensive mode, all of a sudden. A hurt look appeared in her eyes.

"Well," she said, "I'm going to bed if you're in that type of form. Are you coming?"

He shook his head. "No, you go ahead, Angel. I'm going to listen to the wireless for awhile."

"Okay," she replied, bending and kissing him. "Goodnight, then."

"Night," he muttered.

As soon as she was gone he poured himself a stiff brandy. And another. And another. And...

HE AWOKE THE NEXT MORNING with his head pounding.

He hated Mondays.

Angel was asleep beside him. He hadn't slept well, heavy yes, after the brandies, but his sleep had been punctured by tortured cries that he had related to the events of yesterday by the Royal Canal.

He scowled at his image in the bathroom mirror as he shaved and washed. What had he become? His thoughts were so unfocused that he nicked himself shaving, and he held tissue to his face to stem the bright red blood.

He sat on the edge of the bath - morose. His head in his hands.

Reared a catholic he felt the overwhelming desire to confess...to ask forgiveness. When he finally moved it was with a determined purpose.

SINCE THE ARRIVAL OF the Tans into Ireland Troy had found himself at odds with the hierarchy of his church. The Black and Tans were a motley bunch of men. Some were dressed in plain khaki, but most wore a hybrid type of uniform that consisted of dark green tunics, khaki trousers, black belts and civilian felt hats. The Irish coined them with the term Black and Tans after a famous pack of wild dogs in County Limerick. They acted like dogs, snarling their hatred on to the streets of Irish towns and cities, bringing fear in their wake everywhere they went.

They were often drunk. Often violent.

They had been recruited from the ranks of the unemployed in England, and many had been brutalized in the bitter trench wars of Europe. A rumour had circulated in some quarters that they were murderers released from English jails. They alienated even moderate Irishmen - unionists and nationalists alike.

Troy hated them with a passion. As a priest he knew he should have compassion for these new enemies, but the priest found this type of degenerate evil.

FRANK CHURCH DIDN'T like the way things were developing in Ireland.

An astute soldier, he now recognised the Rising of 1916, as a watershed in Irish politics, and he knew it could only be a matter of time before the British withdrew finally from this troublesome colony. The trick though was to stay alive until that happened.

Like many regular soldiers Church had been sickened by the wanton violence shown by the new forces in Ireland - the auxiliaries and the Black and Tans. He had used his power to try and restrain some of the excesses he had seen. The sack of Balbriggan had scarred his soldiering. It had, for the first time, caused him to question his vocation in life. Since an early age he had loved the idea of soldiering, the camaraderie, the crack as the Irish would have called it. He had always led an active outdoor life. As a child he had hiked through the Scottish Highlands and the mountain ranges of England and Wales through his scouting days. The scouts had taught him valuable lessons for his military future.

Practical skills like map-reading, orienteering, surviving in rough terrain. Cooking in the great outdoors. Throughout his entire life he had risen to overcome these challenges...to test his stamina and character and charter against the unknown.

The soldiering had been a natural progression from those scouting days. The army had afforded him the opportunity to travel, to see how others lived. The poverty of India had sickened him, though the place itself had mesmerised him. Egypt had been fun, and he had seen the Great pyramids of Giza, which he reckoned every man should see before they died.

THE POLITICS WERE GETTING to Minnie.

Word had reached her of Shaggy's death. Her grief this time was more tempered...and wasn't anything like the grief she had felt when her husband and son fell at the Somme.

She cried a few tears, but she didn't know whether she was crying for the slain Tan man who had shared her bed, or whether the tears were a simple sign of her own sad circumstances.

Her daughter Mandy came in, pausing when she saw the tears. She had given birth out of wedlock to a baby boy, and it was yet another mouth to feed. Another worry! Mandy's voice was pure Dublin: "What's up, ma? Why are ye crying?"

"Shaggy's dead."

"That bleedin' waster," and then quickly realizing the effect of her words on her mother she went to her and wrapped her arms around her. "I'm sorry, ma," she said, quickly blessing herself, "but he wasn't right for ye. He had a right fierce temper. He's better off out of our lives."

"Do you really think so?"

"Yeah ma, I do."

"But how will we get by?" she wailed. "He brought shillings into the house."

Mandy's face stiffened. "Don't worry about it ,ma," she said. "We'll get by...we always have. What happened Shaggy anyhow?"

"Somebody shot him. They found him in the Royal Canal."

"Well somebody must have had it in for him," she explained. "He was a Tan after all...they're being shot up and down the country."

"Do ye think that's why he was shot?"

"I don't know, ma. He's bleedin' well out o' it now," she explained. "His kind should never have been allowed here in the first place."

"You're so cold, Mandy?"

"I'm sorry, ma. Sorry for ye. But he's left us in the lurch...there's better men out ther' ye'd be happier with."

"Do ye think? Do ye really think?"

Mandy smiled at her mother. "G'wan out of that, woman" she exclaimed. "Of course there is."

LUCY WAS BEING RELEASED.

Her bruises and cuts had healed, and the concussion had been given the all-clear by the doctors. Only the psychological scars remained.

Her movements were slow and laboured as she left the hospital, and she leaned against Ben for support. Physical as well as moral.

A carriage awaited to take her home, paid for by the manager. He had felt it was the least he could do. Inside were bunches of flowers and get well wishes, signed by most of the 's patrons and staff.

She was looking forward to seeing her kids again. They hadn't been to the hospital...she had agreed with Ben to spin them story that she was away for a few days...visiting her sister in England. Neither of them wanted their kids exposed to this type of wanton violence, and they knew that the kids would only have been upset.

They rushed as soon as she came through the door.

"Easy children," Ben cautioned. "Easy. Your mother's had a nasty fall."

Confusion showed on their faces. Cora, the youngest, put all their feelings into words. "Mum. What happened? Why are you limping?"

Lucy smiled. "Stupid me," she explained. "I fell down your Aunt Laura's stairs in England."

That story too had been agreed beforehand with her husband.

She spent the evening talking with her children, and Ben did the evening meal. It was obvious to all that she was still worn out by her ordeal and it came as no surprise when she retired early.

Lucy had a psychological battle ahead of her.

CHAPTER
16

THE CABINET MEETING took place behind closed doors in a safe house. De Valera was proposing an attack on the centre of British rule - the Custom's House. Tony listened with interest to the plans.

His presence at the meeting was testament to the level of trust he had built up with these men. He sensed a tension between Dev and Collins, and between Collins and Cathal Brugha and Austin Stack.

Cathal Brugha had emerged as a real Irish hero of the 1916 Rising, having being wounded twenty five times and living to tell the tale. He had fought with Con Colbert during the Rising. Colbert had been shot by firing squad after the Rising.

Tony didn't know where the enmity between Brugha and Collins originated. Perhaps it was just a personality conflict.

With his journalistic instincts he sensed the politics and undercurrents of tension between the men.

Collins was aghast at Dev's decision.

"Attack the Custom's House," he had exclaimed incredulously. Collin's face was white with fury. "Dev...you can't. Remember the GPO?"

De Valera was adamant. "Our army must act like a legitimate army," he stated boldly. He gave Collins a look that brooked no interference. "Our forces will go and take the Custom's House - the centre of British administrative rule. Perhaps then the world will sit up and take notice?"

Dev won the argument.

Orders for the attack were given.

Collins had been proved right.

The attack on the Custom's House was a bloody fiasco, although perhaps it succeeded in the sense that it shook the British out of their complacency.

Peace initiatives were put out by the British. Dev travelled to London to talk with Lloyd George. When he returned he had a good sense of how far the British could be pushed. He made a report to cabinet.

Plenipotentaries would be needed to strike the deal. Dev wanted balance in the team. Initial proposals included Arthur Griffith, Michael Collins, Cathal Brugha, Austin Stack, and a host of other names involved in nationalistic politics.

London was insisting on the presence of one man. They wanted to meet the man who had wrought such havoc amongst their forces.

They wanted to meet Michael Collins.

Tony made the trip to London at his own expense.

TONY WAS ENJOYING A pint of bitter ale with Collins. His curiosity eventually got the better of him. "What's happening with the talks?"

Collins frowned. "Strictly off the record, Tony."

McAnthony nodded. He sipped at his beer.

"They won't give up the north. Want us to swear an oath of allegiance. We'd have a Free State."

Tony was thoughtful. "Do you think the Irish people will go for that?"

Collins shrugged his massive shoulders. "They might. Griffith wants to sign. So do I."

"What about Dev?"

A sad smile appeared on Collin's face. "That's the big unknown."

"Why isn't he here anyway?" Tony's face had creased into a frown.

Collins took a long sip of beer before replying. "He held talks with Lloyd George already. Maybe he knew how far they could be pushed. Dev's an enigma. I don't fully understand myself why he's not here. He should be here. He's our best negotiator."

Tony was thoughtful. "Perhaps he thinks you're expendable?"

"How's that?"

"It's all politics, Mick. Agreed?"

Collins said nothing. His silence encouraged Tony.

"Maybe he knew how far the British could be pushed. He didn't come to the talks, because he didn't want to be seen as the one selling out on the north."

Collin's brooding silence told him his words had struck home. The Cork man drained his beer with a long sigh. "I'm off," he announced. "Long day tomorrow."

He eyed the journalist before taking up his coat. "You've normally got your finger on the pulse, Tony. Perhaps you're right about Dev. It sounds like him. I'll think it over, but I'm tempted to go along with Arthur Griffith's thinking and sign the bloody thing anyhow. The alternative is a war."

"A Free State gives you something to work with," Tony explained.

"Good night, Tony," Collins said, struggling into his coat. The Cork man left the tavern with a frown on the usual inscrutable features.

There was much to think about. Ireland's fate hung in the balance.

THE TREATY HAD BEEN signed.

Recriminations flew back and forth across the Dail. Some saw it as a sell-out. They saw the north being abandoned to the wolves.

Behind the scenes Michael Collins was conducting highly secret talks with Sir Craig - the Northern Ireland Premier. Dev and his party had walked out from the Dail, refusing to accept the new Treaty. The country was split.

In talks given at rallies, de Valera was talking about 'rivers of Irish blood', and the mood throughout the land was growing uglier by the day. Viewpoints were hardening, and open warfare was being discussed.

FRANK CHURCH SMILED at the women with the wicker baskets who were handing out food and drinks to the assembled soldiers.

Days earlier he had watched the handover of Dublin Castle to the new Irish Free State army. The Union Jack had been lowered, and the green, white and orange tri-colour hoisted in its place. He had never thought he'd live to see the day.

The memory of it was etched in his mind. He knew he had witnessed a truly historic moment. Their orders had come through following the Castle handover - return to England.

The soldiers were happy as they gathered for the mail-boat. They were looking forward to seeing their families. Church was looking forward to seeing his wife Enid, and his two sons, York and Jack. His last furlough had made him wish he'd spent more time back home, his boys were growing fast.

There was rough good humour as the men jostled on to the gangplanks, the seamen aboard fighting a losing battle to stay in control. When he had managed to fight his way aboard Church went to the stern deck and watched as the ship prepared to leave.

Ireland was now free to chose her own destiny, and eight hundred years of occupation had come to a close.

It took some getting used to.

He watched as the Wicklow Hills receded into the distance. On a clear day like today they looked very beautiful. He knew how beautiful the land was up close. He had often hiked the Wicklow Way. The Scalp, Powerscourt with its enchanting waterfall, the glen of Aherlow, Poulaphouca and Glendalough. It was a different landscape to that of England, full of glens and valleys and green foliage. His home country could boast similar sights, but the hiking land of England was mostly made up of heaths and moors.

He had often hiked in Wales, but he found the terrain barren, and the names unpronounceable. He'd take Irish hiking any day of the week.

The boat left a white trail of churned seawater in its wake.

Church turned away, the memory of the land behind leaving an edible permanence etched on his mind, more durable than that of the boat's wash. He wondered when he would visit again. With peace between them, he could now chose to bring his family back with him.

He knew he would be back.

FOLLOWING THEIR INTERNMENT in Frongoch and subsequent release, both Hannafin twins had assimilated back into their lives in Ireland. Both had followed their father into the building trade, finding work rebuilding the city that had been ruined by the shelling during the Easter 1916 Rising. Ciaran had gone down the carpentry route, whilst

Declan had liked the work of the brickie. Bricklaying in particular was lucrative because businesses like Guinness were building city homes for their employees, and the military was also doing the same for their soldiers. Neither lad forgot the struggle for Irish independence, but Ciaran found himself getting more and more involved in the trade union movement; such movements being heavily involved themselves in seeking Irish independence. Ciaran had always been the more moderate of the twins, more open to negotiations with others than Declan.

It was a policy and a philosophy that would tear their brotherly ties apart and test them both to the limit. It was also a policy that would pit them against one another in a bloody civil war that would engulf the nation.

The die was cast!

CHAPTER
17

TONY HAD MADE A REVOLUTIONARY decision.

He had put aside the pen to take up the gun. He looked smart and dapper in his new Free State uniform. He looked at himself in the mirror and wondered again had he made the right decision, but when he looked deep into his heart he knew he could no longer stand aside from the politics affecting his country.

He agreed with Collins that the best way forward was for the Treaty to be ratified, and he was ready to back up his belief with force of arms and concrete action. It was a decision every Irishman and Irishwoman was being forced to review.

His revolutionary style of journalism had brought him to this point. Since the Rising of '16, his beliefs and ideals had been constantly challenged, and he could no more have ignored the coming fight than he could his own parentage.

Because of his education and background and the fact that he knew many of the top men he had been given the rank of captain in the new army. It was a position he would revel in.

He knew war could only be a matter of days away. The British were exerting pressure on the new government to act against the Irregulars. The newspapers were saying that if Griffith and Collins didn't act then London would intervene.

That was the big fear of the day.

Nobody wanted more intervention by the British. There had been enough intervention from that quarter throughout the centuries. It was unthinkable that they'd interfere with Irish politics yet again. No sane Irish person would want that.

Irish freedom had been won at a price.

The price was Irish blood.

The signatories of '16 had not been the first to shed that blood. Earlier rebellions, in 1798 and 1803 and 1867, had extracted their share of true Irish blood. But the signatories of '16 had proven the playwright Yeats right when he declared: "All has changed utterly." The men of the Rising had kick-started the current process, and although most of them had paid the ultimate price, their ideals and visions were about to be realised.

Tony could see that. It was the principle reason he had laid aside his pen in favour of the gun.

He had a meeting arranged later in the day with Angela. He wondered what she'd make of his decision? He decided he would look his best. He would wear his uniform to their meeting.

"TONY? WHAT ARE YOU doing wearing that uniform?"

Tony grinned. "Like it?" he commented.

"No, I don't bloody well like it," she snapped.

The grin slid off McAnthony's face. Jesus, he'd never understand women. What had he done wrong now?

"What's wrong with it?" he snapped back, his good humour disappearing fast.

She stared at him, her dark eyelashes flashing with fury. "You're a journalist," she said. "Not a soldier."

"Things change, Angel."

Her fury was astonishing. "Tony, you're fighting on the wrong side. That Treaty isn't worth the paper it's written on. Can't you see that?"

So she was anti-Treaty. Tony hadn't thought of that. He had thought she would fall into line with whatever he thought was best. How wrong could he have been? He wondered now why he hadn't seen the signs earlier. The slight barbs in her tongue whenever he mentioned Michael Collins or Arthur Griffith.

He should have realised earlier. Kerry had always been a strong Republican area, but even if he had guessed her true allegiances, her vehemence was still surprising. Her voice was like a whiplash, as she heaped scorn on his new look.

"Sure, what do you know about soldiering," she snapped. "And killing."

"Enough," he commented quietly.

"You write. That's what you do. You know nothing about killing."

"Have you forgotten the GPO?"

"What about it?" she snapped. "You had no part in the fighting. You sat on the sidelines. Your weapon is your pen."

Her anger was so intense. "The pen is mightier than the sword," she mocked.

He lost his cool. Told her something he shouldn't have. "You were mighty pleased when Lucy's attacker was found dead, weren't you, love?"

"What do you mean?"

"How do you think that Tan ended up dead? So fast after the attack?

"You had him killed?"

"I killed him."

She stared at him in shock. "Why did you never tell me?"

"What was the point?" He was still angry.

She lapsed into silence. Still sullen. When she looked up, a decision had been reached in her eyes. Her words were cold - like ice.

"Michael Collins is a traitor," she said. "So is Arthur Griffith, Cosgrave, O'Higgins. They all sold us out. Our relationship is over, until you come to your senses. I never want to see that uniform again. I'm going home for a few days to Kerry. If you get rid of that uniform, you know where to find me."

"Don't you think you are over-reacting, Angel? Our marriage has nothing to do with these events."

"I've said all I'm going to, Tony."

He watched as she stormed from his apartment.

GENERAL MICHAEL COLLINS gave the order for the eighteen pounders to open up on the Four Courts. The Four Courts were an impressive concrete building, designed by Thomas Cooley, and finished by Gandon, and was named after the four courts of the land. The District Court, the Circuit Court, the High Court, and the Supreme Court.

His heart was heavy.

These were men he had trained and fought with, but all his behind the scenes manoeuvring had failed to make an impact. The Irregulars who had taken control of the Four Courts complex last week had refused point-blank to vacate. The Free State was under pressure from the recently departed British establishment to take action. Take action, or we will, was the unspoken comment. Nobody wanted that. The British had been involved in Irish affairs long enough. Nobody wanted them back.

His closest ally - Harry Boland - had taken the Republican side. De Valera had stirred the country up since his walkout from the Dail.

Moderates and the church had fallen in behind the Treaty. The newspapers were also backing the new government under President Griffith.

Die-hard republicans like Oscar Traynor, Liam Mellowes, and Cathal Brugha had decided to take on the Free State. Their numbers were powerful.

The British had given the Free State artillery pieces in which to put down the uprising.

The Irish Civil War had begun.

THE NEWSPAPERS WEREN't slow to denounce the growing menace of Irregular snipers operating in Dublin City. They rapidly fell in behind the government of the day.

It was a far cry from their stance during the Rising, with one publication denouncing the Rising as "utter madness".

Tony was now directly involved in the fighting. In the distance he could hear the cannon as they battered and pounded and shelled the Four Courts. Slivers of rock and cement sliced into the defenders. He could see the plumes of smoke hanging over the city. Tony and his men fought from roof to roof, flushing out the Irregular snipers who were exacting a heavy toll on the citizens of Dublin.

A shot caused Tony to duck his head, but the sniper's aim was off and the bullet whipped slivers of stone from the wall behind him.

"Get down," he screamed at his men.

One of his men spoke from the corner of his mouth, his voice harsh, strained. "Where did that fucking shot come from?"

"Fucking snipers," another man muttered, a cigarette dangling from his lips as he scanned the rooftops with cold eyes. The soldier lifted his rifle and fired suddenly.

"Got the bastard," he exclaimed, and all of the men heard the clatter as the fallen Irregular slid from his roof perch.

"Nice shot, soldier," said Tony, standing up. He gave orders to move out. "Keep your eyes peeled," he warned.

The men moved from rooftop to rooftop, checking constantly for booby-traps and snipers. Snipers always had to be killed. It was too dangerous to try and take them alive.

The war was getting dirtier by the second with each side giving no quarter.

Irishmen were fighting Irishmen.

CHAPTER
18

THE MEETING TOOK PLACE in Skerries.
Collins had wanted to see the place where Harry
Boland had met his end. He was accompanied on
the trip by Dick Mulcahy and Pairic O'Toole. Skerries was a seaside port, off the road that led north,
and surrounded by low-lying hills. Boats lay at
peaceful anchor behind the pier wall, as the men enjoyed a rare pint. Mulcahy didn't drink alcohol - he
had a pot of tea in front of him.

A few Free State troops lounged nearby, soaking up the sun's rays, but their eyes were alert. Their Lee Enfields lay nearby, stacked against a chair.

Collins took a sip of his beer and looked around with appreciation, but not without a little sadness in his tones. He gazed at his two companions, his hazel eyes suddenly sad. "You know, Harry spent a lot of time out in this place."

The three men lapsed into silence, thinking of old times. All three had been touched by this war in some way or another. Collins suddenly dropped a bombshell. His two companions looked at him aghast.

Pairic suddenly exploded. "Damn it, Mick. You can't go. It's bloody suicide. You'll be walking into your own grave."

Collins smiled. "Pairic, my old comrade, you're a brave man. I remember how well you fought alongside Pearse in '16 and survived to tell the tale. They were our comrades, and yet they accepted death as part and parcel of the struggle. As I must do if I'm to have any hope of bringing a peaceful solution to this bloody mayhem."

Pairic glanced at Mulcahy. "Talk some sense into him, Dick."

Mulcahy shrugged. "Mick's his own man, Pairic. He'll go to Cork regardless of what I say."

Pairic didn't like it. For no reason whatsoever he was suddenly very suspicious, and apprehensive. He was adamant in his protestations. "It's a bloody trap. They want to get him in his own backyard. They might figure he'll have his guard down."

Collins was equally adamant. "And what if Dev is genuine, Pairic? What then? Maybe he wants peace as much as we do."

"On his terms, I bet." Pairic's voice was sour.

"Pairic, you're too cynical. This war of attrition has hardened you. You're too blinded by hate to see the possibilities that might arise from this opportunity."

Mulcahy spoke up again. "It's not like that, Mick. Pairic hates this war as well as every other decent Irishman. You know that? Don't forget his loss...it's just he's concerned for your safety. We all are. He might be right, you know? What then? It may well be a trap?"

"Trap or not. I've got to go. I owe it to the Irish people. To do any less, would be to besmirch the Treaty, I returned from London with. I've got to find a way of accommodating Dev's wishes with our own ideals. Otherwise we're all doomed."

Pairic wouldn't let it go. He took a long sip of his beer and called in his round. "It didn't work before," he stated. "What makes you think Dev and his republicans have softened their attitudes?"

Collins shrugged and sipped his beer. "There's been too much blood shed. Too many deaths - needless deaths. Arthur Griffiths was proof of that."

"We're all sorry about Arthur, Mick. This war broke his heart. But Dev and them will never swear allegiance to the Crown or give up the north."

Mulcahy nodded in agreement with Pairic's words.

Collins sounded angry. "Good God, man. Do you think I want to relinquish our legitimate claims on the north. Hell no. But we've got to work at it from a position of strength. Not weakness."

"They won't listen...," Pairic began.

"They've got to listen," Collins replied, with quiet steely determination, his anger subsiding. "We've all got to live on this island. It's imperative a peaceful solution is found."

Pairic's suspicions were aroused. "Who advised you on this approach, Mick?"

"The Cabinet were very supportive. McFry in particular had some good suggestions."

"I'll bet!"

"Why that tone of voice, Pairic?"

"McFry isn't a good strategist, Mick. His loyalties might lie elsewhere."

Mulcahy's eyes narrowed. He hadn't known Pairic had doubts about McFry.

Collins too expressed surprise. "Why's that? Because he was once close to Dev, Oscar Traynor and the rest of the Volunteer Executive. I won't buy that, Pairic. We've had this argument before. He's as dependable as any man we've got."

"What about the GPO?"

"What about it, Pairic? We were hopelessly outgunned. We'd no choice but to surrender."

"True," Pairic agreed. "But he done some of the negotiating, remember? With General Lowe."

Lowe had accepted the surrender from Pearse.

Pairic was still arguing. "What we were promised? Not what we got?"

Collins nodded. "We lost good men. I know."

"All the signatories."

"Except Dev," Mulcahy added.

"Exactly." Pairic looked at them both.

Michael Collins was slowly shaking his head. "Are you suggesting, Pairic, that McFry negotiated a separate deal for Dev?"

"He had very powerful American links...very like Dev, in fact?

Collins and Mulcahy looked troubled. It was an aspect of the affair they hadn't considered much before. Pearse had sent a nurse to negotiate with Lowe, but Collins suddenly remembered that McFry had conducted his own negotiations.

They drained their pints.

New worries had set in.

TONY HEARD FROM MULCAHY that Collins had gone to Cork. He was surprised.

"What's he hoping to achieve?"

Mulcahy shrugged. "He was always against this war. You know how he felt about Harry Boland. He thinks he can talk Dev around."

"There's no hope of that. Things have gone too far. Didn't you tell him that?"

"There was no talking to him...he insisted on going."

"It will be dangerous for him down there."

"Agreed. But he took an armed convoy with him."

Mulcahy gave him new orders and Tony left his superior's office with a tight frown on his face.

A nagging feeling of worry was beginning to envelop him.

DE VALERA WAS ALSO a worried man.

He was now on the run. Out on a limb. Dublin had become too hot, and he had retreated south through the country to Liam Lynch's hangout in Cork. Secretly he was tired of this war. His mind was always active, discarding option after option, and wondering how to end this bloody mess. He was still grieving for his friend - Harry Boland. An Irregular came up to him, and told him Michael Collins had been seen in the area a short time before.

"What?" Dev had grabbed the man, excitedly.

"We're going to ambush him, if he comes back this way." The Irregular grinned.

De Valera was suddenly aghast. He grabbed the man again - violently. "You can't do that," he exclaimed, in a horrified tone.

"Why not?" The man shook off his hand, and gazed curiously at de Valera. "The man's our enemy."

"He's here to negotiate," explained Dev. "You can't kill him."

"If you've got a problem with this, see Lynch about it."

"I will," said Dev grimly. He stalked off, shaking his head at the folly of men.

Lynch was no better than his men. He heard Dev out, but he insisted that he was in charge of this region, and that if Collins returned to this area, his men would be waiting for him.

Dev couldn't believe his ears. "Liam," he pleaded, "this war is going against us. We have to consider the possibility of surrender."

"Surrender!" Lynch laughed harshly. "Nobody's surrendering on my patch. If you don't want a part of this, then stay out of our way." He swivelled to face his men. "You men have your orders. Get moving."

"Don't," said Dev, but he was pushed aside. He retired to his room, seeing there was nothing he could do to dissuade them. He was absolutely furious. He brooded. His mood was suddenly melancholy.

How had things degenerated so fast? He wondered.

He recognised that he may have made the wrong decision in not going personally to the Treaty talks in London. His mood darkened as he thought of this. He lay on his bed. Thinking. He drifted into sleep.

It was growing dark when he awoke. He could hear voices downstairs. Somebody approached his room and knocked. It was one of Lynch's men. A rifle was slung over his shoulder. He eyed Dev warily and said quietly: "He's dead. Thought you'd like to know."

That was hard news to take. "Dead? Mick Collins?"

"Yeah."

Dev hid a groan. He turned away, indicating by his silence he wished to be alone. With Collins gone, Dublin could get very dirty. The Free State government would be furious. Collins had been a friend once, and perhaps always had been, and he had definitely been a moderating influence on the more hardline elements within the new Dail. Dev recognised the simple truth of that. He guessed that with Collins gone, things could very ugly indeed with this war. He would be lucky to survive this mess himself. He was surprised at the grief he felt.

Next morning he left Lynch's hangout with an eight-man team and headed cross-country to Macroom, ignoring the incessant chatter of Lynch's men, alone in his thoughts and wishing to be left strictly aloof. He left Lynch's men in Macroom, and travelled onto Limerick, and then onto Dublin, staying in safe houses all along the way. Dev could be a master of disguise and at various times he pretended to be a farmer, a travelling salesman, and once even as a vagabond.

He stumbled forward.

Dublin beckoned.

"THEY'VE BROUGHT IN Emergency powers."

Dev swore. He knew that the Free State government would take tough action in response to the death of his erstwhile friend Michael Collins. He had just been briefed by one of his top men in the Irregulars.

He realised the man was still speaking. "It's imperative you stay out of sight Dev and keep a low profile. They're scouring the country for you. My sources tell me they searched Binn Eadair the other day...looking for you. If they'd found you? Well, lets just say you wouldn't be here talking to us."

"Why Howth?" Dev asked.

The Irregular grinned. "Little bit of misinformation we managed to plant. Don't worry, though. You're safe here."

Word of the reprisals hit Dev's ears later. Men had been removed from their cells in Kilmainham, lined up against a wall and shot dead by a firing squad.

The war had turned very dirty indeed.

The news from Cork was shattering.

Michael Collins was dead. Dead at the age of thirty-one. Ambushed by a party of Irregulars in his own home county of Cork. Bael na mBláth, they were saying.

A silence had descended upon Dublin City when news of the tragedy broke. Tony was as shocked as anyone else. He wanted to lash out. What was it Collins had said upon his return from London? It was the best they could get. A stepping stone to the Republic.

Tony just couldn't believe it. He was still grieving, and reeling from the shocking death of Arthur

Griffith a week before. Harry Boland's death had also come as a shock. August was proving to be a bad
month.

And now this.

He sensed now that the Civil War would only
get worse. Their best chance of peace lay dead, shot
by a sniper's bullet.

CHAPTER
19

THE WAR HADN'T BEEN going well for the Irregulars. Many of their strongholds had fallen. Harry Boland had been shot dead out in Skerries. They
still had formidable fighters - men like Liam Mellowes, Kale, and Lynch; to say nothing of Dev; but
they were nonetheless on the run. Rattled.

The government was standing behind the Treaty
as negotiated by Collins and Griffith, and General
Mulcahy who had taken over the army was issuing a
plea for 'no reprisals'.

Tony sensed though that the government was incensed by the death of Collins, and from this point they would harden their attitudes.

Since donning the uniform of the Free State Army, he had felt his own attitudes hardening. This was to be a war with no quarter given. The Irregulars had to be put down, and put down fast. He felt no pity when he heard of reprisals. They were on the wrong side. Death was the penalty for calling the play wrong.

But Tony also had a quandary. If Republicanism was wrong, then where did that leave Angel?

She espoused the very tradition of Republicanism. She'd lost a brother in the Tan War. Could he go against the woman he loved in pursuit of what Collins had described as 'a stepping stone to a Republic'? Tony didn't know, and was afraid of the answer.

He knew that he had a strong love for his country. He also felt that the Treaty was the best way forward. He sighed heavily.

IN GALWAY AND SLIGO men crossed themselves when they heard the news, and one or two even took to their oars and their curraghs to pass the word to the outlying Islands - the Aran Islands. All along the mighty Shannon the news spread like wildfire throughout the midlands. Up in the north, men reflected and commented: "Ah, sure, wasn't he a wee Irishman afterall. A great Irishman." They took it hardest in Dublin. In places like Wexford and the southeast they felt sadness.

Only in the rebel counties of the southwest - Cork and Kerry - were the harshest words spoken. "Him and that bloody treaty...sure didn't he sell out the north. He made his bed...let him sleep in it. He reaped what he sowed."

In Kilmainham jail up in Dublin, one thousand Irregulars, got down on their knees and said the rosary in Irish. Though enemies of Collins and the

Free State they recognised the tragedy of the moment.

Frank Church had made good on his promise to return to Ireland. He had been in the country for several months now working as a military observer with the Free State army, and liaising with London to provide the new army with advice, logistics and arms. His rank was now that of Brigadier, having being promoted from Major to Lieutenant Colonel and then Colonel. His hair had receded with the passing of the years and with the extra responsibility command thrust upon his shoulders. When news of Michael Collin's death reached his ears he felt intensely sad for Ireland, recognising the fact that the country had lost a great statesman. The sadness was felt on a personal level too because more than any other man he had worked very closely with the Corkonian. He had seen at first hand how the effects of the Civil War were tearing the man apart. When the news broke, Church had been conferring with the prison governor of Kilmainham Gaol and he saw firsthand how the Irregulars got down on their knees to a man and prayed for the soul of Michael. He watched in stunned silence as they prayed in their native tongues;

An tÁivé Máiria—The Hail Mary

'Sé do bheatha, a Mhuire, atá lán de ghrásta,

tá an Tiarna leat.

Is beannaithe thú idir mná

Agus is beannaithe toradh do bhroinne, Íosa.

A Naomh-Mhuire, a Mháthair Dé,

guigh orainn na peacaigh,

Anois agus ar uair ár mbáis. Áméin.

"Would you look at that?" the governor breathed.

One of Church's entourage, a British captain, muttered darkly: "Fucking Irish. I say, I'll never understand them."

A look of annoyance and exasperation appeared on both the governor and Brigadier's faces and Church rebuked his officer. "Watch your language, soldier," he warned the man.

The soldier made a face but said nothing. He was one of a handful of officers the Brigadier had brought with him from England. The man had seen service in Ireland previously and had witnessed the excesses of violence wrought by Republicanism. He understood Irish politics but he viewed it with a jaundiced eye.

The kneeling Irregulars were still on their knees, completing the decades of the Rosary in the Irish language.

Church crossed himself.

JOHN TROY TURNED THE sacristy key with a sure-fire click.

It was important that the door remain tightly closed. His mind was full of turmoil, because he knew he was breaking church rules. But what was a man to do? Stand by and watch his country suffer?

He wasn't made like that. All his life he had prided himself on the fact that he was a man of action.

He had always taken the hard road in life. He had few regrets. He was intelligent enough to realise that not every answer lay in prayer, or if it did it remained well hidden from the mortal eyes of Father John Troy. He had prayed for guidance and in the end he had trusted to his own conscience. If a man couldn't trust his own conscience then there was something seriously amiss.

Throughout the troubled history of Ireland, men of the cloth had always taken a stand. Some did no more than preach from the pulpit, but their views carried weight. Some took up the pike and led the battlers on, as had happened back in Wexford in 1798.

Though he didn't agree with the Irregulars, Troy found himself unable to turn the other cheek when they came to him looking for help. The three men, men from his own parish, were on the run and feared an early morning execution if taken alive. Troy had explained his thinking to them and they had heard him out in respectful silence. The older of the three then butted in quietly, despair in his tones. "Then you won't help us, father?"

Troy had looked at the three men in turn. He shook his head slowly, knowing that his refusal would break these men. He knew them all. He knew he could shatter any faith they might have left in the church with his next words, but he wasn't the type of man or priest to turn these men away. His voice was equally quiet when he replied: "I'll help you," he said. "I've said my piece. What do you want me to do?"

The older man had grinned. "Hide our guns. If we're caught with them, we're dead. And we need to disappear for a time."

Troy pursed his lips thoughtfully. A friend of his managed a monastery in Glendalough, Wicklow. The three men would be safe in hiding there. They needed to pretend they were men of the cloth. Monks. He knew a tailor in Dublin who could help with that bit. He explained his plan.

They liked it.

The guns were the biggest problem. He decided to hide them in the sacristy. Later he could have them buried in the vaults. He consoled himself with the thought that by offering succour to these desperate men he had removed three guns from the fighting which raged like a devil over his beloved country.

He wasn't aware that he was being watched as he hid the guns. McGinley's smile was pure evil.

THE FUNERAL OF MICHAEL Collins took place in the Pro' in Dublin.

His body had left Cork by sea, and had been shipped back to Dublin where it had lain in state in City Hall. The streets of Dublin, and even the rooftops overlooking the streets were awash with people paying their respects. Virtually all of the men wore hats - trilby and derby hats, tophats, and assorted hats and country caps which they removed as the funeral cortege went by.

Tony stood watching the proceedings in the warm August sunshine. He reckoned some half a million people had shown for the event. The coffin had been lain out on a gun carriage following the service in the Pro, bedecked with flowers and floral wreaths.

As he watched events unfold, Tony's thoughts were very much on estrangement; not just the estrangement that death could bring, but on the very real pain of separation and he wondered for the umpteenth time what Angela was doing. He lit up a cigarette, drawing heavily on the smoke, his mood pensive and sober.

Other men were in the shadows, and like Tony they were watching the proceedings unfold. The Cloak was there, and so too was the former intelligence officer Harry Sword. Both nodded to each other but didn't converse, both wrapped in thoughts of the man they had known.

Ireland had changed irrevocably.

The two Hannafin brothers came face to face over bayonets in a fire-fight near the Coombe. Brother against brother.

The Coombe was an old area of Dublin with narrow streets and cobbled alleyways.

Declan Hannafin faced Ciaran Hannafin and didn't fire. His face showed shock.

"Ciaran?" His shout startled his brother, who also paused.

"Dec?"

Declan's face edged into panic, aware that his own troops were behind. "Get out of here, brother."

Ciaran's face was stubborn. Ignoring his brother he lifted his rifle at a Free State soldier behind Declan, but before he could fire, he staggered back, hit by a shot. His rifle fell, and he clawed a handgun from his pocket.

"Ciaran," said Declan, his face paling when he saw his brother's wound. He dropped his rifle and ran and supported his brother. He tried to reach the revolver, and wrest it from his brother's grip. "Give it up, brother."

Ciaran smiled but didn't release his hold on the revolver.

Declan heard the warning shout behind him to get clear and he cried out: "Don't shoot."

The Free State troops had no choice.

Ciaran Hannafin was levelling his revolver at the troops behind Declan, and was ignoring all warnings to drop the weapon.

The Free Staters opened up.

Both brothers were hit.

Ciaran Hannafin saw the blood stain Declan's Free State uniform, and his face changed. His eyes lost their stubborn look and he opened his mouth to say something, to say sorry, he hadn't meant for his brother to get shot. He realised he should have dropped his revolver, and he dropped it now. A look of fear darted into his eyes, not for his own safety, but for that of his brother.

"Dec," he gasped, "you're hit."

Declan didn't reply. His grip on his brother tightened in a spasm, and Ciaran's eyes glazed over as he realised what had happened.

"No," he muttered. His lips had gone cold.

They died in each other's arms.

The soldiers approached slowly, warily. Bayonets at the ready. Fingers on their triggers.

They looked at their own man. One man cleared his throat awkwardly and growled: "Why didn't he shoot him?"

Captain Pairic O'Toole stared down at the inert face of Declan Hannafin, whom he'd known for years. His revolver dangled limply in his hand - unfired. He knew all the Hannafin clan. He cursed softly, bitterly, as his keen gaze fell on the other man's face.

Suddenly he was sick of this war. When he spoke his voice was as soft as a sibilant hiss and his men had to strain to hear him.

"They were brothers."

MINNIE'S FAMILY WAS coming apart at the seams.

She wasn't sure how much more of this she could take. Her daughter Mandy had been right on one point - it had proved relatively easy to get over the death of Shaggy. But new problems continued to dog her life.

One of her sons had been locked up in the 'joy. "Stealing with menaces," the judge had said, looking out into the public gallery and briefly catching her eye. "Seven years," he had said, making her almost want to scream her anguish at him. She had bit her tongue instead.

Mountjoy Prison was a bleak, dark bricked incarceration centre in Phibsboro, and a place she despised visiting. She detested the stench of the place, the intrusive body searches every time she went to visit her second eldest - now the eldest since Jimmy had died on the Somme with Jim Senior - the whispers and the nudges, the cold stares of the screws.

Then she found out Mandy was hanging out around the Monto, selling her body, using her woman's body to bring in cash to the home. This time she had screamed, screamed her rage at her daughter.

She had been wondering for months how her daughter had so much cold cash. "What are you doing girl," she screeched. "How could you?"

Mandy had blushed red with shame. She hadn't wanted her mother to find out. Her voice was defiant when she replied: "Get real, ma. What chance has a girl like me...no husband...no job...tied down with a kid."

The young woman had stood, hands on her hips, daring her mother to speak. It was all too much for Minnie. Sobs racked her body.

Mandy felt her heart relenting, but she was still angry. Angry with her mother and with the world. She stormed out, slamming the door behind her.

If she had stayed perhaps she could have done something to prevent what happened next. Minnie remained sobbing on the couch, and when she finally stood she felt a moment of weakness. The pain hit her like a sledgehammer in the chest. She gasped, sudden tears of shock in her eyes.

There was nobody there to catch her falling body as it hit the stone cold floor. Dead.

In the corner the baby cried for its milk.

ONCE AGAIN, TROY FOUND himself officiating at a funeral mass in the Pro'. The mass for Minnie was full of people from the tenements. It was a good showing, and Minnie would have been proud of the turnout had she been around to see it.

Her favourite hymns were sung by the Palestrina choir high in the loft. Amazing Grace, What a Friend we have in Jesus and How Great Thou Art. The soothing tones of the choir helped to drown the grief of the family below.

After the burial the family retreated to their local pub. The pub was the crutch that supported the broken legs of the Irish. It was there in times of happiness and of sorrow. It was an institution.

LUCY'S FRIENDS HAD helped her to recover from her ordeal, perhaps none more so than Tony McAnthony.

She still had nightmares about that night but they were becoming less frequent. The business of living had also helped her to recover, looking after her husband and children, and the counselling had helped.

A big factor in her recovery was knowing that her nemesis was dead. Somehow there seemed to be a poetic justice in that, an air of melodrama like she had often seen played out on the stages of the Abbey Theatre. She could walk the streets of Dublin again, her head held high. She allowed nothing to hold her back or to dent her newfound confidence.

It was a feeling she liked.

Billy Hannafin greeted Pairic O'Toole at the door of his tenement, but a look of trepidation and fear appeared on his face when he saw the expression on O'Toole's face. O'Toole told him about Declan and Ciaran, and their last stand together. Billy staggered under the weight of the news and stood staring blankly at Pairic O'Toole's face. When he spoke his voice was a bare whisper.

"Dead? My two boys?"

O'Toole stood awkwardly just inside the tenement hall door, aware of the keening noise arising from the women within, and wanting to be anywhere but here at this spot right now. Billy Hannafin's face had aged suddenly and he looked very vulnerable, like a man about to have a stroke.

"I'm sorry, Billy."

"Jesus, Mary and Joseph," cried Billy Hannafin. He reached blindly for the chair behind him, sobs racking his body as he tried to come to terms with the staggering news. O'Toole stepped forward and placed a reassuring hand on his shoulder.

"How did it happen?" Billy had regained a measure of control. "They didn't..." he started fearfully, "each other?"

O'Toole shook his head. "It didn't happen like that." He realised that Billy was worried that somehow, one or both, had killed the other. They were on opposite sides of this conflict nonetheless.

Billy's eyes were hopeful.

"They died together. In one another's arms. Declan died trying to shield his brother."

"Thank God," Billy cried out. A brief smile lit up his face. "In one another's arms?" He made the sign of the cross.

"Yes!"

"This fucking war..."

"Tell me about it," O'Toole said, with equal bitterness. Pairic O'Toole had also lost a brother in the first week of the conflict. His brother, Sé, had been killed in College Green by an Irregular sniper.

"Will it ever end?"

"It will end, Billy."

"Where are my boys?"

"They were taken to the morgue at the Richmond."

"Let's go," Billy said, standing up, and struggling with his coat. He comforted the women of the house before leaving the house with Pairic. Neighbours were gushing out of nearby tenements alerted by the women's sobs and screams.

"What's happening?" one woman asked.

"The Hannafin boys are dead."

"Sweet mother of Jesus...the Hannafin boys. Declan and Ciaran?"

"Yeah," her neighbour confirmed. "They would have been twenty-one next week."

"Oh, God bless them. Will this bloodshed ever end?"

"Who knows, Frances," her neighbour said. "Perhaps some day...but for now Joyce will be needing us.

The neighbours steeled themselves before approaching the Hannafin doorway.

"YOU'VE HAD ENOUGH?"

Mulcahy stood staring at the younger officer, his face working with inner turmoil as he digested Pairic O'Toole's words. He needed this man. Good fighting men were hard to find. He understood men like O'Toole too well. He knew the man wasn't bottling out, that he had guts. Mulcahy sighed deeply. Sometimes he wished Michael Collins were still around. He motioned to the chair on the opposite side of his walnut table.

"Sit down, Pairic."

He gazed at the younger man's troubled countenance. "Want to tell me what's troubling you?"

Pairic fought back sudden tears. "It's this fucking war," he exclaimed. "Brother against brother, Irishman fighting Irishman." He told Mulcahy about the Hannafins, about Declan and Ciaran, about the weeping women, and of how he'd stood in awkward silence as Billy Hannafin gazed down at the inert faces of his sons in the cold morgue room of the Richmond Hospital.

A long silence ensued when he had finished. War took its toll on every man. It burnt out men on every front. It hardened them and made them immune, impervious, commanding. And very, very cold. It was a brutal business, often with no quarter given, because in this crazy world it was dog eat dog, kill or be killed, fight or get sucked under into a deep morass of peat-like swamp bogland. It was bitter and bloody. Tough and bruising. There was little room for emotion, and the killing was carried through with an unrelenting passion, climaxing in a sea of blood and guts. It was obvious that O'Toole had enough of the killing. The expression in his hazel eyes was bleak. His mouth was tight, uncompromising.

Mulcahy cleared his throat. Eventually he broke his silence: "I can see you need a break, Pairic. Don't quit yet. Take some time. I need you, man."

Pairic shook his head. His voice when he spoke was very sad, very emphatic, and very final. "I'm finished!"

THERE WAS A TRUISM spoken in the 'joy that if you had a skill you kept your mouth shut about it. If the prison authorities lashed onto the fact that you were a skilled chef, carpenter or any of a hundred different trades, then those skills would be utilized to the fullest extent possible and you'd serve every single day of the sentence handed down by the courts.

The way that things broke for Troy though was that he had no need to open his mouth. His case had been well publicized and everyone knew he was a priest even without glancing at his collar.

The governor of the 'joy was delighted and immediately set up an interview with him. He was a rotund individual, with bright inquisitive eyes hidden behind thick spectacles. He was reading Troy's committal warrant when the priest entered. He waved absent mindedly at the chair as Troy came in, and he dismissed the accompanying prison guard. Finally he looked to Troy with a friendly smile. "Father," he acknowledged. "Court documents say you'll be with us for a year or so. I'm sorry to see a man of the cloth in this position, but now that you're with us, perhaps we can make good use of your talents."

"Talents?"

"Yes...you're spiritual skills." The governor was silent for a few moments. "Rome hasn't defrocked you or anything like that...you're still a Roman Catholic priest...are you not?"

"Still a priest," Troy confirmed.

"Excellent!" The governor beamed. "I'm not going to give you the usual pep talk...about how good behaviour can increase chances of remission of sentence...you're not a hardened criminal or anything like that...so, I'll skip all of that. You won't find the 'joy totally unpleasant...men make mistakes in life and they end up here. It's a question of class. Many of our prisoners here come from what we call deprived areas, poor areas, if you will. I'm sure you've dealt with these types before?"

Troy nodded his agreement.

The regime of Mountjoy prison would take its toil on the nationalist priest.

Things would change irrevocably.

THE FUNERAL OF THE Hannafin twins was a heart breaking affair.

Both coffins had been draped with tri-colours. Both would be honoured with a firing party. Pairic gave a brief oration, at Billy's invitation, telling the mourners how the brothers had died together, in each others arms, each shielding the other. Joyce Hannafin broke down during the ceremonies and had to be supported throughout.

When the echo of the three volleys had died away, Pairic turned away.

He hoped never to hear that sound again.

Riflefire!

THERE WERE PRIESTS in the diocese that recognised John Troy as a good pastor who really looked out for his flock - the parishioners within the Pro's confines. They knew him to be an upright, brave and honest individual, even if he was somewhat outspoken on key events. They knew he had used the pulpit to get his nationalistic message across, and they feared he had gone too far with his views. Over time they had drifted away from the man, fearing that if they stayed too close, they too would go down when he inevitably fell.

The hierarchy in Dublin and elsewhere in Ireland could be very powerful when they wanted to be. Troy had made powerful enemies within the church, and it was rumoured that even Rome was unhappy with their outspoken priest.

Warnings were handed down to Tuite. "This is your responsibility...sort it out." The warning was more in what was not said. "Don't make us step in."

Rome's feelings on the subject were reinforced when the Papal Nuncio, effectively the Holy See's ambassador in Ireland, reached out to Tuite and told him in no uncertain tones to get his house in order.

Tuite was no fool. He could see the writing on the wall. He had failed to control his people. His career upward had effectively stalled. He decided to call a meeting of the Irish hierarchy, men only too willing to attend, men with an axe to grind, men who knew how to shaft a young, outspoken priest who had shown them all up at one time or another.

It was payback time!

A RUNNING GUN BATTLE was taking place over the terrain of the Knockmealdown Mountains.

South Tipperary and the border county of Waterford. The screes were brown and barren looking, with a few sheep the only longterm residents.

The fight had turned for the Irregulars. Their strongholds had fallen like knights on a chessboard. Limerick, Wexford and Cork.

The brilliance of Michael Collins had won through. Elements of his infamous 'squad' had invaded key positions from the sea. Drogheda had fallen.

Pockets of resistance still existed though, and Tony's command had been ordered to wipe out any resistance.

He had ordered his men to spread out, and they fanned out on the lower slopes. Intelligence sources had indicated that leading republicans like Liam Lynch and de Valera were in the area.

Tony had orders to apprehend them.

Shooting broke out on the slopes. A running gun-battle.

Liam Lynch went down in the same way that had struck the mighty Cathal Brugha back in Dublin - with his guns blazing defiantly.

More gunfire erupted from higher up the slope, and the Free State troops sent a wicked fusillade of shots towards this new threat. A scream of pain, a woman's squeal, shattered the evening air, and the men held back firing more shots.

One look at Liam, told Tony that the man was finished. He wasn't dead yet, but he soon would be when they attempted to move him. His eyes scouted ahead, peering through the descending gloom to pinpoint where the other gunfire and scream had erupted from. He scrambled up the scree slope, his handgun out.

The woman was face down on the brown earth. He turned her. Blood saturated her back. Tony dropped his handgun and throwing back his head, he shouted out a long-drawn cry of agony and pain.

Angela's eyes flickered in recognition and she stared accusingly at the weapon on the ground.

Numbly he shook his head. "It was my men," he said, flatly. He remembered the time in the GPO when she had administered him as he lay bleeding, and knew from looking at her blood saturated uniform that he couldn't do anything except to hold her.

He could tell she was dying. He pleaded with her. "Hang in there, Angel. I'll get help."

"It's too late, my l...love," she grimaced, her breathing ragged and shallow. "I'm very cold."

Blind panic appeared in Tony's eyes and he hollered for the unit's medic. He held her in his arms, aware of the lifeblood seeping his uniform, urging her to hold on.

The sudden convulsion and spasm shook her and smiling sadly into his eyes, she died.

Tony wept.

His men found him huddled over her body. They didn't understand. Some guessed and crossed themselves. They gazed down in pity.

They had to virtually carry their commander away. Tony was comatose.

WHEN THE MIND IS GRIEF-stricken, the body seems to recognise that fact. Tony stared out from the apartment towards the sea, his eyes seeing nothing but the past. His heart was heavy within his chest and he smoked continuously. He hadn't eaten for days. He ignored the growls of his stomach.

He had seen to the details. He couldn't attend her funeral. It was a Republican stronghold, and although he knew Jonjo and his family wouldn't have lifted a gun towards him, he had agreed with Jonjo that it might be best to stay away. Angela had had too many friends.

He had said his goodbyes in Limerick Junction where a train was waiting to take her on her final journey. He bent over the coffin and kissed her cold lips, and touched her cool forehead. He didn't feel right about leaving her. His uniform still held patches of dried blood. He wasn't aware of that.

His men waited for him outside the carriage, their voices low and shocked. Those who had answered Angela's fire with fire of their own, now wished they had held back. Many had never wanted this war. There were people on both sides of this conflict reluctant to fire on one another.

The men were sick of it. They wanted to go home. They wanted to be with their families. They wanted an end to this mess.

They prayed for an early settlement.

Tony prayed for a miracle!

None had come. In the end he had returned to Dublin with his men. Mulcahy's orders. In light of his circumstances he had been relieved of command, and ordered to take what time he needed. His troops had been stood down.

New reinforcements were being rushed to Kerry to mop up the last of the rebel strongholds.

For Tony McAnthony the Civil War was at an end. It meant nothing anymore.

THE SQUAD ACTED AS troubleshooters for the Free State, and they were an elite unit attached to the army of the Free State. The four man team lifted Enda McFry in a lightening swoop on his home as he left his dwelling for work. They ignored the pleas of Susan who saw what happened from her kitchen and came running out to help defend her husband. They swept her aside and bundled Enda into a jeep, tying him up as they did so. They blindfolded him to confuse him further. Two of the men jumped into the back of the vehicle with Enda, and the other two jumped into the front. As they drove, Enda tried not to think what all this meant. His captors remained uncommunicative as they swept along, answering his questions with monosyllabic grunts. It wasn't a good sign. They drove along what seemed like city streets, judging by the sudden turns, general activity and sounds of the tram. When they arrived he was bundled out of the vehicle in the same unceremonious fashion, led down some long corridors and thrown into a very cold room. It felt like an icebox. Enda shivered. The floor felt like stone beneath his feet. Some kind of cell, he surmised grimly. They left him there for what felt like hours. He wondered what Susan must be feeling.

And then he smiled, suddenly realizing what course of action she'd take. She'd campaign for his release. He could almost see the scene in his mind's eye.

Many women might have sat down and cried their eyes out in the circumstances that Susan McFry found herself in, but Susan was made of sterner stuff. She could have sat down on her laurels and played a waiting game but she wasn't made like that. She loved her husband and she wanted him back. The thought of living her life without Enda by her side made her want to retch; nor did she want to sit down with their two little girls trying to explain to their sweet innocent faces why their daddy wouldn't be coming home. Ever!

No way. She immediately reached out, contacting everyone she knew. With a woman's intuition she guessed that the snatching of her husband had something to do with the assassination of Michael Collins. A staunch member of Cumann na mBan like Angela O'Sullivan, she had also helped with Ingrinidhe na hEireann, and she had numerous contacts from both organizations that she immediately reached out to.

She was put in touch with the renowned Dublin journalist who upon hearing her story agreed to write up a spread covering the kidnapping and an appeal to return Enda McFry safe and unharmed. He also promised to use his military contacts to try and ascertain what might have happened to the political advisor. Like Susan, he had the feeling that the kidnapping was somehow related to Michael Collins and he promised to do what he could.

The campaign to release McFry had got off to a good start with good people brought onboard, but Susan still refused to let up. She began a personal

crusade, carrying banners outside Dail Eireann, campaigning tirelessly for the release of her husband. She
attracted media attention and they agreed to carry
her story, and her high profile protest outside the
gates of the Dail meant that several prominent TD's
wanted to hear her tale of woe. She was joined in her
protest by other women of the Cumann who never
forgot the sacrifices made by former members. Her
campaign was gathering pace.

Enda endured some questioning at the hands of
the squad, but he was surprised after a few days when
three men entered including their leader, a man with
the name of Vincent, and proceeded to untie him.

Vincent stared at him with cold eyes and commented: "You have important friends and that wife
of yours..."

"Susan...is she okay?"

"She's fine," Vincent assured him, lighting up a
cigarette and surveying the political advisor through
a cloud of smoke. "She must love you a lot. She never
stopped."

"Stopped what?"

"Campaigning on your behalf," he replied, blowing another cloud of smoke towards the ceiling. "You're free to go."

"How come?"

Vincent finally smiled. "Didn't you hear? The Civil War is over."

WEEKS DRIFTED INTO months.

He had grieved days and nights. A deep melancholy made all his movements listless. His inner sadness tore at him. He was drinking heavier, a fact he wasn't proud of. He had never sought answers at the bottom of a whiskey bottle before, and he hated himself for his weakness. He was also chain-smoking. He knew what Angela would have said. He remembered the night he had the row with her...the day he had killed the Tan who had raped Lucy...the day when Michael Collin's 'squad' had been turned loose on Lloyd George's men...the day when the

Tans had retaliated by butchering people at a GAA match in Croker.

Four years ago now!

Sometimes it seemed like yesterday. On other occasions it really did feel like four years. Where did time go?

His work lay forgotten, his movements growing more listless.

Some days he had gone for long walks, lost in his own thoughts, retracing the steps they had taken together. He could see her smile in his sleep. In his nightmares.

The walks were helping him to recover. He liked walking along the seafront in particular, especially on days when the saltwater lashed his face and stung his eyes. He wondered what the future held?

One day he arrived back from one of his long walks to see a familiar figure waiting on his doorstep.

Jonjo O'Sullivan had aged considerably. He didn't look well. Tony was shocked by the old man's appearance, and he had a sudden insight that the

Kerry farm man was clutching to life and was just barely hanging on. The man's countenance was as pale as white birch, and he looked close to collapse.

Tony had gripped him by the arm, concerned lest the old man fall. "You should have told me you were coming to Dublin," he griped concerned. "Have you been waiting long?"

"Not long," Jonjo ground out.

Tony ushered him into his apartment and helped him sit down. The loss of Henry and Angela had taken all of the fight from the old man.

"You'll have a small one?" Tony offered.

"Aye lad, I will." A brief coughing spasm racked his body.

Tony poured two glasses. Neat scotch.

He raised his glass to the old man's.

"Sláinte," he said. "To your health!"

"And yours," Jonjo replied. He took a gentle sip, relishing the taste. Then he glanced at Tony. "I'm sorry, you couldn't come to the funeral. You'd never have got out of there alive." He paused, and coughed.

"The Kingdom was the last stronghold, ye know? A touch of Kerry pride touched the old man's tones.

"I'm sorry I missed it, Jonjo." He sipped his whiskey. "How did it go?"

"These things are always hard," he replied. "We sang her favourite hymns...I think she would have appreciated it."

Tony sighed heavily. "You know there's no words..."

Jonjo waved his pipe, silencing him. He eyed the journalist with those wise old eyes. "She loved you, you know? She never stopped talking about you...she was always happy when you were around...she wouldn't want you wallowing in grief."

There was a powerful truth in the old man's words.

Tony remained silent. Thinking.

"You didn't see her when the two of ye broke up...that foolishness over the colour of your uniform...how miserable and broken-hearted she was."

"But it still happened," Tony said bitterly.

"It did," said Jonjo. "These things always happen in life...believe me? You made her happy, Tony. Nobody else could have. Never forget that."

"But why did she go against me?"

"Look boy," Jonjo pleaded, "I'm getting on in years. Wouldn't think I have too many years left...at least, I hope not...not after...". He struggled to get a grip, lighting up his pipe. Inhaled the deep Virginia tobacco with pleasure. "But you," he continued, "you've got to move on...take life by the scruff of the neck and carry on...for Angela's sake as well as your own. Live your life, Tony. Don't spend it looking backwards, regretting the past. Do ye see what I'm saying to ye?"

"I do, Jonjo," Tony replied quietly. "I'm glad you came."

The old man didn't reply. He seemed deep in thought. Eventually he looked up.

"Are you still in the army?"

Tony shook his head. "I left...after Knockmealdown."

"That would have pleased her," he observed. "She always felt you were the better man when handling the pen rather than the sword." There was another hesitation, as though he were concerned...

Tony sensed his reticence. "What is it?"

Jonjo's face was strained.

Tony reached forward and placed his hand on the old man's shoulder. "What's wrong? What is it?"

"Angela."

"What about her?"

"She was carrying, Tony."

"Carrying?"

A tear escaped the old man's eye. "An unborn," he said. "The doctors told us afterwards...I thought you'd want to know."

The shock hit Tony like a sledgehammer. "Was it...was it?"

"Yours?" The old man looked at him in pity. "I knew her too well, son. There was never anybody else. Never. The baby was definitely yours."

Long after Jonjo had shook hands with him and left the house Tony remained sitting in the same chair. Sobs racked his body. He stared at the far wall. Unseeing. When eventually he moved he felt like an old, old man...worse than Jonjo.

He moved to his writing study and looked at the US postmarked letter he had received that morning. A job offer from the States. A new beginning. A place where he could maybe bury the heartache and do as Jonjo had suggested. Take life by the scruff of the neck and just get on with it.

The other alternative was to tear the envelope in two and drink himself into an early grave. When eventually he turned to leave the room the envelope lay undamaged on his writing bureau.

THERE WAS A SAYING spoken of in the 'joy that if you had a skill you kept your mouth shut about it. If the prison authorities latched onto the fact that you were a skilled chef, carpenter or any of a hundred different trades, then those skills would be utilized to the fullest extent possible and you'd serve every single day of the sentence handed down by the courts.

The way that things broke for Troy though was that he had no need to open his mouth. His case had been well publicized and everyone knew he was a priest even without glancing at his collar.

Day in, day out, Troy practiced his faith for the prisoners, but the truism was the bitter truth. There was no early remission for those with skills, not even for Roman Catholic priests.

Troy had to soldier on.

TROY HAD BEEN SUMMONED to the archbishop. He wasn't long out of prison having served every single day of his sentence, his features still carrying a gaunt look and the scars of incarceration.

Things had changed over the years. No scones or pots of tea awaited his arrival. He had become something of a pariah, an embarrassment to the hierarchal order that watched over Mother church in the Irish Free State. He removed his long trench coat and tapped his long fingers impatiently against his trouser leg. What the next hour would bring, God only knew, but Troy had reached a plateau in his life, and he was no longer content to sit by and watch his people suffer.

When Tuite entered the room, it was obvious that it wasn't just Ireland had changed in the intervening years. The Archbishop's face was haggard and drawn, and deep trench-like lines marked the older man's complexion. His voice was dull when he spoke, with little hint of the earlier magnetism and fire, and the figure was more pronounced and more stooped than when Troy could last remember. Pity moved him to try and help the old Archbishop, but the man swung his crozier like a band conductor, and shrugged away his help. He eyed the younger man grimly with his grey eyes.

"You've been making lots of enemies, John."

"God's will!"

The Archbishop smiled tightly. "Or John Troy's will? He paused, before adding: "Suppose you heard about McGinley?"

Troy nodded, remaining non-committal.

Shocking thing, Tuite was saying. "Who'd want to murder a Catholic priest?"

"He obviously made enemies somewhere. Maybe he should have let well enough alone."

"Bad enemies, to carry out such an atrocity. The newspapers made him out to be an angel."

"Perhaps he wasn't the choirboy they all made out."

"Huh. What do you mean, John?"

"You know he was friends with Simmonds, Darcy and Black. They called them the Four Horsemen of the Apocalypse."

"No. I didn't know that." He paused for a few minutes before adding: "You know I've been getting worrying reports on Darcy. Rumours that he's mess-ing around with children in the parish. Young boys. Altar boys, would you believe?"

"What are you going to do about it, Ray?"

Tuite wringed his hands. "Rome wants me to sweep it all under the carpet. But I'm going to retire the fucker," he announced decisively. "Can't be putting up with that kind of behavior in my parishes."

Troy restrained a grin. Tuite's use of foul language was unusual and showed how perturbed he was by the allegations. There'd be hell to pay.

Troy didn't rise to the Archbishop's bait. He wasn't going to make it easy for them. He had served his church for twenty two years now, and he knew he was about to be shafted. There were too many powerful alliances arrayed against him...though one or two still supported his views...and he was not without friends within the church, including Rome.

To give the man his due, the Archbishop didn't beat about the bush. He was very forthright, and perhaps, but arguably plausible. "We need to evaluate your career, John?"

"We do?"

"Yes."

"Who's the we?"

The Archbishop didn't respond to that one. Instead he gazed shrewdly at the younger cleric, and wondered why a wedge had been driven between them? He recognised the sadness of the situation, because he remembered the good times. Times when he had shared this man's confidence, and times when he had trusted the younger man's judgement. But those times had gone - the mists of time had clouded a lot of issues. Time had moved on to a new plateau - a somewhat dangerous platform of shifting allegiances and loyalties. He was wise enough to know it was all politics. When he spoke Tuite's voice reflected the hard decisive nature of his thinking: "Given the choice, John," he remarked, "where would you like to move to? Where do you see yourself ten years from now?"

"Are you serious?"

"I'm very serious."

Troy remained silent. Thinking. Like Tuite he also recognised it was about politics - a game. Where did he see himself in ten years? It was a good question, a worthy question. A slow smile spread across his face.

"Why are you smiling?" Tuite asked.

"I can pick anywhere, right?"

"Within reason," Tuite cautioned. Rome would be out of the question. Rome was a base from which power emanated. The new forces within the church would never agree to Rome, in case the young cleric harnessed that power and came back to haunt them. That would never do.

"How about America?"

"Why America?" Tuite asked surprised.

Troy shrugged. "It's a place our people have always gone to. Exiles. I've family over there - another big plus."

Tuite considered the matter, relieved that the young cleric hadn't mentioned Rome. But America? He hadn't envisaged that. It was far enough away to please the younger blood within the powerbase of the Irish church, far enough away that their swords might not cross again. It was now Tuite's turn to smile. He should be able to swing that one.

"Leave it with me," he advised.

"One condition," Troy added.

"Which is?"

"The east coast. New York...Boston, perhaps?"

Tuite agreed. It was a reasonable request. He stood to go and hesitated. Too much had passed between them for it to end like this. "John," he began hesitantly, "can we part as friends, at least?" The older man held out his hand to be shaken.

Troy looked at the hand for a long moment, and for a long drawn out moment Tuite thought he would refuse to shake. But the moment passed, and the familiar boyish grin appeared on Troy's face and he said: "Sure."

The two men shook hands. It wasn't because of the deal they had just cemented, but was a sign of an earlier friendship, a friendship that had been broken like Ireland had broken the chains to her colonial past, and a friendship that had been torn apart by the maelstrom that constituted Irish political and church life today.

"I'M SORRY TO SEE YOU go, Father."

Billy Hannafin had arrived at the Pro-Cathedral to pray and light candles for his two sons, and bumping into Troy had struck up a conversation with him. Troy had just told him he was moving to America.

The young priest eyed the building labourer who espoused everything this church stood for. He could see the damage the Civil War had wrought on the man's features - the haggard, grief-stricken look, the haunted air of unreality, and the anguished torment. He smiled at Hannafin.

"Thanks, Billy," he said. "How are you coping?"

Billy shook his head in despair. "Not too good, Father."

"Time is a great healer, Billy," said Troy.

"Yeah, I know that."

"And Joyce...how is she coping?"

"She wants us to move, Father."

"Where to?"

"England. London."

"That might not be a bad idea, Billy. New surroundings might help with your grief. There's also plenty of work over there in the building game. Would you not consider it?"

"I am considering it."

"Do it, man," Troy advised. "What have you got to lose? If it doesn't work out, you can always come back."

"Will you pray for me, Father. That I do the right thing."

"Consider them said, Billy," Troy assured him.

Billy smiled, the smile lighting up his face as though a candle had flared near his eyes. He grasped

Troy's hand. "I'll pray for you too, Father...that you're doing the right thing?"

Troy shook hands with Billy Hannafin. "That might not be a bad idea, Billy," he said sincerely.

"Luck to you, Father."

"And to you, my son."

PAIRIC O'TOOLE WAS burning his uniform.

He had lit a fire in his back garden, and the flames matched the setting sun in the sky, giving his face an orange glint as he kept his eyes fastened on the glow. He had a pitchfork in his hands and as the smoke rose, he used the fork to feed his army uniform to the flames.

The threads in the material caught immediately. The burning stench caught the back of his throat, and he moved his head away. His hazel eyes followed the smoke skywards. His thoughts followed the tendrils of blackish smoke, and he wondered to himself what to do now?

Going back to the army was out of the question. He had spurned all attempts by Mulcahy to reconsider. O'Toole had never married, though he was still a young man, and there was still time if that was what he wanted. He wasn't sure it was anymore. Since the deaths of the Hannafin twins his mind had been over-reactive. Something had changed within him.

He felt the same exact feeling he had felt on the morning of the Rising...that a new chapter was about to open in his life. The start of a great new adventure. He had been speaking with the Franciscan order for weeks, and he had gone on a couple of retreats with them - holy places like Glendalough and Gougane Barra in Cork. The peacefulness of these types of surround had cleared his mind of the violent images he had been seeing for the past six years.

The violent life he had been leading had given him much pause for thought...they'd hardly want a man like him? But he had never revelled in the bloodshed...had in actual fact despised it. His vocations director had told him about St. Paul and his conversion from violent ways on the road to Damascus. The story had resonated within him...giving him pause for thought...making him empathise with that historical figure of two thousand years ago. They had given him time to make up his own mind. Time to heal the wounds within him. The time had come though to make his decision.

The fire was burning down to its final embers and he noticed the chill wind which followed the settled sun. All he had to do was go to back into the house and pick up a pen...accepting that it must be God's will.

He watched the embers for awhile. Then he put his fork away, back into his tool shed. When finally he entered his house, he strolled slowly to his desk and picked up a pen. The life of a Franciscan lay before him. He had never being one to shirk a challenge.

THE CIVIL WAR HAD FINALLY finished.

It hadn't been a very long war, unlike the American Civil War that had lasted four long years some sixty something years before, but it had been a very bitter one, and like all wars very, very costly.

Those who came out of it on the other side were glad to have done so with their lives. Many hadn't, and the bitter legacies it had spawned would spiral down through the years in further outrages. But for most Irish people, the war had expunged their bitterness and they were glad it was over. They were also glad they had their country back. The British were gone...and they had something to build on now. They would sow the seeds for future generations of Irish people.

The problems for the Irish people now were in some respects problems they had grappled with in yesteryear. Emigration was still a harsh fact of life. America, Australia, New Zealand, Canada, and even England - they all seemed to offer a better way of life. It would take years of struggle before Ireland could be truly free. Free from the shackles of the past...free from the horrors of the Famine, which some of the elder generation still remembered and which had displaced and killed millions of Irish...free from the heavy emphasis which had always been placed on agricultural produce...free to produce new goods in a market driven economy. There were definitely challenges ahead.

The mailboats had always run a service between Ireland and England. Many an Irish family had emigrated that way. The boats ran constantly between ports in Dublin and ports in England and Wales - Liverpool and Holyhead. Billy Hannafin gathered his family around him, the boys struggling with the heavy cases, and they crushed onto the gangplank together. Some able seamen hurried to help them, and Billy thanked them profusely.

Once aboard they crowded into a large saloon, and Billy went up on deck to watch as the ship left Dun Laoghaire. Joyce joined him, slipping her arm around his waist.

"Sad?" she asked, her own voice a little downcast. They had gathered yesterday at Glasnevin cemetery to say a final farewell to Declan and Ciaran, and they had invited neighbours in last night for a final drink. Billy had expressed surprise at Pairic's decision, his eyes widening in disbelief, before grasping the old soldier's hand and wishing him well. In age terms Pairic was still relatively young, but in soldier's terms he was old - the horrors of war evident in his eyes and bearing.

"A little," he said, leaning into her. They could see the Wicklow Mountains receding into the distance, a gentle mist hanging over them, giving them a haunting, surreal view. The bay of Dublin had been swallowed up by the churning waters of the Irish Sea. Seagulls cackled overhead, hovering over the railings at the stern. They seemed to be laughing.

"Let's go below," she said, eventually. She looked deep into her husband's eyes before turning away: "It will work out, Billy. Trust me!"

"I do," he said simply. He hugged her to him as they went in search of their children.

ENDA AND SUSAN MCFRY were delighted when the Civil War ended.

Susan had been particularly concerned about her husband, because in the wake of Michael Collins getting killed, she had heard recriminations and veiled threats against Enda's life. And of course, that had nearly come to fruition when he had been kidnapped, but it was behind them now. She knew her husband too well though. She knew he had been distraught at the death of the Cork man. He had been particularly anguished, she knew, because it was partly his advice which led to Collins taking that fateful journey.

The advice haunted him.

It woke him out of deep slumbers, sweating and afraid, and Susan had to use all her powers to persuade him to relax...to try and forget the tragic events of Bael na Blath. She had felt a surge of relief in the days following the assassination, and a sense of gratitude at the magnanimous remarks of Richard Mulcahy in the press that had called for 'no reprisals'.

She knew within her heart that if this plea hadn't been made that her husband might have been taken out, placed against a wall, and shot. She was under no illusions about that. Mulcahy's orders had been obeyed to the letter.

They had not gone to the funeral per se, fearing further angst, but they had stood among the Dublin crowds lining the cortege route and had paid their respects that way. The grief hadn't been a surprise, Collins had won over the hearts of Dublin a long time ago. His picture adorned many Dublin homes, often alongside images of the Sacred Heart.

With the war's end, Enda had thrown himself into parliamentary work. It was work he excelled at. Susan had gone back to lecturing.

They were excited about the new future.

Ireland had won her freedom, and they both felt they had a contribution still to make to society. They spoke openly of starting a family...they shared a new confidence about the future.

They had won a number of battles, both personally and professionally. The future had never looked so bright.

HE HAD GONE TO SEE Lucy.

"Life isn't the same without her, Tony."

"Tell me about it."

"She loved you. You know that, don't you?"

"We were going to have a baby," he said. "She never said...but Jonjo came and saw me after the funeral."

Tears appeared in her eyes. "Oh, hon," she sympathized. "I'm so sorry."

"So am I."

There was a long silence. Eventually Lucy flicked her eyes up at him and said: "Tony, there's something I have to ask you?"

"What's that, Lucy?"

"That time when I was raped...Angela told me you had taken care of that animal...the rapist. Is that true?"

McAnthony's face clouded over. "I'd sooner not talk about that, Lucy."

"Please," she said. "I have to know."

"It's not something I'm proud of," he said. There was an undertone of pain in his voice that she recognised, but she had to make him understand.

Her voice was small when she continued: "That night," she shuddered. "It was the worst night of my life. That pig followed me...forced himself on me. He ripped all my clothes, and f...forced himself into me, and then when I struggled he beat me within an inch of my life. I'm glad you got him, Tony. Ben was glad too."

"Please Lucy," he pleaded. "It's all in the past. Why rake it up?"

"Because I need to know for sure," she said vehemently. "Just to stop the incessant nightmares I keep having about that animal...what I don't understand, Tony? Why you? Why did you go after him?"

"It needed to be done," he stated flatly. "Why me? I don't know Lucy? Perhaps because I was to hand? Perhaps it was because of the effect on Angela. Who knows? I set out with the intention of finding him...not killing him. The killing was an afterthought. He was a Tan. They'd never have put a Tan on trial. Not even for a hideous rape. I wanted justice...and I knew the right people who would help me to accomplish that."

She drew close to him, and kissed him on the cheek. "Thank you," she murmured. She didn't care what his reasons were any more. He had explained the impulse that had driven him to kill that day.

"So, what now Lucy? How are you coping now? Are you getting counselling?"

"Life goes on, doesn't it Tony." Her voice was sad, reflective of the past. "I've received some counselling...but it's hard to erase the memory."

He nodded his head in agreement. "You've got lots of things to look forward to," he assured her. "You've a good husband...you'll see your kids growing up."

"Yes," she agreed. "There's always positives." She looked at him with concern in her eyes. "And how about you, Tony? What does life hold for you now?"

"I'm putting all this behind me, Lucy. Starting afresh. I got a job offer from the United States."

Her breath caught sharply. "You're going away?"

"Yeah. I'm going to America."

She smiled. "Angela would have liked that...she wouldn't have wanted you retreating into yourself. I'm glad, Tony. Glad for you, and glad for her memory. When will you leave?"

"I've settled most of my affairs here now," he said. "I'm going next week."

"Will you write...let's us know how you're getting along?"

"I will," he promised.

She bit her lip, suddenly thinking that here was another good friend gone. But she couldn't deny she was happy for him. "So Tony," she said, "this is a goodbye?"

"It is, Lucy. I'm not great at goodbyes, so say farewell to Ben and the kids for me."

She approached him and hugged him tightly. "You take care, Tony...take good care of yourself."

He held her for a moment and then released her. He winked and gave her his familiar grin. "Goodbye, Lucy," he said, and turning he left the room.

PAIRIC FELT A STRANGE sensation as the doors of the abbey clanged shut behind him. In a way it was like shutting the door on his former life, and the bad things that had been associated with that life.

He had given away what few possessions he had. He had no regrets.

The old friar who ran the order had taken him to a room and had ordered him to change into a brown habit. He donned the coarse garment, with its hanging crucifix, and slipped into a pair of sandals. His surroundings were austere; stone cold floors, simple furniture. He would be joining the other friars for matins, and then a welcoming meal.

Before leaving the room he glanced at his appearance in a small mirror. His reflection grinned back at him.

He hardly recognised himself.

CHAPTER 20.

TONY LEANED OVER THE railing of the White Star liner as she left Queenstown bound for New York. A tricolour blew in the breeze at the helm of the ship. His heart was very heavy.Crowds lined the decks waving goodbye to those on shore. Many had tears in their eyes. The steep waves of the Atlantic were beginning to heave the ship up and down, but Tony remained where he was, and wondered for the millionth time where it had all gone wrong.

His love was dead. Angela. Life didn't seem worth living?

Killed in a skirmish in the closing days of the Civil War. He hadn't been able to save her. In the end she too had given her life for her version of a free Ireland, despite her beliefs being at odds with Tony's. He wished he'd tried harder to convince her. He was a highly trained journalist, with strong negotiation skills, honed by years of experience, but still he hadn't managed to convince her to his way of thinking.

Fucking Irish politics, he thought bitterly.

He remembered their last encounter, the way her eyes danced, the sweet curl of her ever-smiling lips.

It wasn't a totally happy memory. They had argued.

Bitterly.

"They gave up the north, Tony," she had said. "What kind of Treaty was that? Pearse would turn in his grave."

"You don't know that, Angel."

Her eyes had flashed. "I do," she exclaimed vehemently. "Tony, this is driving us apart...don't you see that?"

"I can't see why you're so driven on this. Collins claimed that it is a stepping-stone to a Republic. Can't you see that?"

Her eyes were downcast. Sad. She said nothing.

He tried another tack. "In years to come they'll do away with that Oath of Allegiance...mark my words. Are you listening, Angel?"

"I'm listening."

"But not hearing," he said angrily.

Her eyes flashed with anger of her own. "This whole Treaty is wrong," she said. "Dead wrong. Why should Ireland have to pay war costs to England? Swear an Oath to their Crown. I'd rather be dead," she spat.

He was taken aback with her venom. Where was the woman he had fallen in love with? Why couldn't he get through to her?

He wanted to plead with her. To beg, almost. Pride held him back.

"Is this it?" he asked plaintively. "Is this how everything ends?"

"You should have stayed with journalism, Tony." Her voice had softened, and a tear glistened in the corner of her eye.

"Angel...", he began, but paused when she held up her hand. She put her finger over his lips to silence his words. Puzzled he waited.

She removed her finger and leaning forward gave him a lingering kiss, before pulling back and saying: "Enough. Goodbye, Tony."

He had lost her.

It showed in every fibre of her being.

Angered he watched her go. His anger dissipated as soon as it had appeared. He waited for her to look back.

She didn't.

He wanted to follow her. He felt paralysed. Was this how things ended? Love?

Perhaps she needed time. He consoled himself with the thought that she would return. When she had time to think.

Time however had run out for both of them. Time was their enemy. Time would run out for many an Irishman and woman during the Civil War.

The ship was picking up speed. Increasing its knots.

Yards from Tony, another man looked longingly at the land he had grown up in. How had things degenerated to this? he asked himself. He too felt bitter.

Ireland was his land.

What was so wrong in wanting a free country? Why couldn't his superiors in the church have taken a more hard-line approach? Why did they always have to sit on the bench?

Troy's heart was very heavy.

He was leaving his land behind. He'd grown up in Ireland, and had spent most of his life there, except for periods when he had been training for the priesthood and had went to live in both Italy and Israel. On shore people were waving from the harbour of Queenstown.

He felt the first stirrings of seasickness as the ship moved in motion with the stormy waves. He stayed on deck.

He glanced around. Surprise registered in his eyes as he recognised Tony McAnthony.

The recognition was mutual.

Both men nodded.

Tony smiled sadly. "Ironic isn't it, Father. She won her independence and freedom and now we're both leaving."

Troy had to agree. "Is Angela not going with you?"

A film of pain crossed Tony's face. "Didn't you hear, Father. She's dead."

The shock registered in Troy's countenance. He had liked that young woman. "How did that happen? And when?

"Eight months ago now," Tony said reflectively. "She was killed in the Knockmealdown Mountains with Liam Lynch."

"The republican?" Troy asked, immediately blessing himself and muttering a silent, final prayer. The battle over the Knockmealdowns had been one of the last actions of the Civil War, the priest realised. What rotten luck!

Tony nodded.

Both men were silent for a few moments. The shoreline was becoming distant. People had started to clear the decks and go to their cabins below. "And you, Father. What's your story? Why are you leaving?

"The hierarchy didn't like my rebellious thinking. They decided to transfer me."

"I'm sorry."

"Don't be, Tony. I'm better off out of it. They've given me a new parish in New Jersey."

"Sounds off the beaten track?" Tony commented.

Troy smiled grimly. "They want me out of the way, I suppose. Too outspoken for them...anything to shut me up."

Both men fell silent again. The bow of the ship cut into the ocean waves, slicing them apart. The rise and fall of the ship was now very noticeable. Deckhands scurried about performing various tasks. The thoughts of both men turned to the new land - America. Scores of Irish people had already made the same journey.

America beckoned. Exile!

About.

An Irish writer with professional qualifications in journalism and visual media, the author has self-published several books, including The Soaring Spirit, Kolbe, The Briefcase Men, Wings, Digger, Land of Our Father, and recently The Scribe. The author has a Facebook presence at Liam Mullen Author. His titles are available on Amazon and Kindle and Smashwords. He also has many stories on the go at Wattpad. He currently lives in Wexford.

The idea for The Nationalists came during a lecture on the history of the media when studying for a journalism degree. The story has been enjoying some success on Wattpad and has attracted a number of readers. It's currently a Wattpad featured story. Testimonials from readers include: "Bloody accurate." HusnaM.

"A wonderful read that takes the reader back in time and into the heart of the rebellion. This story is giving the heroes flesh and blood; they are no longer just figures from history." Museshack.

"Excellent read." RichardLamison.

"I've only just started this, but so far I'm enjoying it greatly. I think you perfectly recreate the atmosphere and mood at the time. Additionally as someone with strong Irish nationalist heritage I find this incredibly interesting anyway. Well done! I can't wait to continue reading this." livstar1.

"I cannot explain how much I adore this. As an Irish person with personal family history relating to events you've written about, I think you've dealt with the history very well. And I'm proud, and immensely happy, to be able to read about it. You've done our history a justice with your writing. Thank you." LaurenDumbrowski.

The author is grateful for these acknowledgements of his work and thanks everyone who has taken the time to read his work. It is envisaged that the book will be one of a trilogy. Book two will be entitled Exile and will focus on the Irish experience in America, and the third book will focus on the sixties and seventies.

Coming Soon: War. In a time of war, nobody's innocent. A compendium of short stories, some with an Irish slant, focused on the theme of war.

An extract.

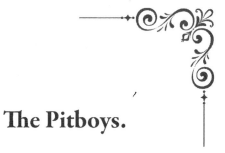

The Pitboys.

"MAKE SOME BANSHEES, boy." The fireman's tone was uncompromising. "I'll rig the cane in, and you two lads clear the area until the smoke clears. As soon as it clears, start filling the buckets with coal again. Clear?"

Hennessy, the older of the two lads, bobbed his head. "Clear, sir."

In any other country but Ireland, Michael 'Mickey' Hennessy and his companion, would have been at school, but the country was just emerging from the savage ravages of a potato famine, and things being what they were, far from normal, even thirteen year old boys were being pushed out into

407

the workforce, the niceties of school forgotten as they laboured in the mines beneath Ballingarry in County Tipperary. Michael regarded himself as a tough lad, but even he found the labouring conditions a bit on the rough side.

One nice thing was that they were no longer regarded as boys, but as working men. They still wouldn't get a pint at the local inn McGillycuddys, but they were treated with a newfound respect. Work had that effect. It brought the money in for the bread and butter. It also brought sage advice from some of the older heads: "Don't get too used to this type of work, lads. It's backbreaking, dangerous toil and it will eventually tell on your health." The two lads would nod in agreement, fearing to contradict what the older men were saying.

Mickey's companion, Birdy Finn, grinned at him as they emerged from the coal shaft. "You look like one of those black babies the schools are always collecting for."

Mickey grinned. "So do you."

Nobody knew how Birdy had gotten his name, perhaps it was his fluttering fingers which at the moment were ingrained with black soot from the coal. He was a small lad, somewhat stocky as opposed to Hennessy's lanky slight frame. On a hot summer evening they'd often sit on barrels outside McGillycuddys and watch the world go by. Most of the women wore shawls and the men usually wore peaked caps. Some of the children went around barefoot and looked with envy on the sturdy workboots worn by Mickey and Birdy, one of the few perks of the job. From their vantage point they could hear the raucous laughter of their older workmates as the effects of Guinness and Paddy's whiskey took hold.

It was in and around McGillycuddys that they first heard talk of insurrection. Rebellion was in the air, not just in little old Ireland, but all over Europe. Earlier in the year, a revolution had broken out in France. Such events were heard of usually through 'word of mouth', and through the few newspapers that circulated at the time. Newspapers were normally ferried about by canal barges and men on bicycles.

It was at Ballingarry that the pitboys first saw the Irish tricolour unfurled - the green, white and orange fluttering in the wind. It looked magnificent. It was an image of freedom that they all secretly longed for. No peoples liked to be under the dictat of another nation and for too long the English had ruled over Ireland with a mighty fist. Ireland had had to endure savage repressions by the likes of Cromwell who had left his bloody imprints in the minds of the Irish. It had also suffered under the penal laws, and Irish children had been taught in hedge schools. It was a nation that yearned for its independence. That it would come at some point was a point on which they were all agreed, but just when was a point of contention.

There was a man in town that the pitboys had often observed. It was known that he'd broken away from Daniel O'Connell's Repeal Association and had started his own movement, a group called the Young Irelanders. The man's name was William O Brien.

Travelling from county to county, Kilkenny and Wexford mostly, trying to drum up support for his new movement. He had what the Irish called the 'gift of the gab', and Mickey reckoned he must have kissed the blarney stone at some point in his life because he came out with fine rhetoric. He could get a rise out of the crowds that flocked to hear his words...of that, there was no doubt. The Irish Constabulary kept close tabs on him, but they would, wouldn't they? They were the eyes and ears of her majesty's crown forces. Sharp eyed peelers with the Queen's shilling in their pockets who cared nothing for ideal notions like Irish independence. Their lives were made up...thank you very much.

O'Brien despised them, and it showed in his speeches. He was often seen in the company of two other men - John Meagher and Richard O'Gorman. All three men were earmarked for special monitoring by the Constabulary. It was suspected by the forces of the crown that the three men had travelled to France to observe first-hand the effects of the French revolution. The authorities had them down as dangerous revolutionaries, men who by the force of their personalities could influence the pitboys and others of a rebellious streak.

The pitboys heard the gelignite explode and made ready for the coal shaft again. The next few hours would be busy ones. They would need to shore up weak areas of the shaft with puncheons or chocks, before loading more buckets of coal into the 'bogey' rail cars.

It was hard, tough work in subhuman conditions: little light, no sunshine, and every movement had to be measured to prevent caving in. The coal itself, as one of the older hands delighted in telling, was dirty and filled with dust. The older hand knew all about the stuff: the anthracite with its high calorific value and low ash content, black coal, hard coal, stone coal, blind coal, Kilkenny coal, crow coal, craw coal, and black diamond. Mickey reckoned he was a right expert when it came to coal. He had to wonder why Dingle didn't have the fireman's job, such was his love for coal. Perhaps they knew he had shaky hands, earned from the illicit trading in poteen that he made near his home in the Slieveardagh hills. He was another one under constant scrutiny from the peelers, but for different reasons.

With the day finished they went home to their respective houses. Both lads were bone tired. "See you, Birdy," said Mickey.

"Bright and early in the morning," Birdy confirmed.

Mickey smiled and strolled on. His reverie was interrupted by a quiet call of his name. "Got a minute, Mickey?"

He recognised the man as a sidekick of O'Briens. He went by the name of Finnegan and Mickey knew him to be trouble. He tried to avoid the encounter. "Not now, Harry," he said, trying to skip aside.

The man moved to block his progress and Mickey frowned. "Best make the time, Mickey," Harry warned.

Mickey sighed. "What do you want, Finnegan?"

"Your help."

"Help with what?"

Finnegan didn't answer directly. "Understand you're working the mines now?"

"What of it?"

"You've got access to explosive on that job," Finnegan explained. "We could use some of that."

Mickey shook his head. "It's under lock and key. Only the fireman has access."

"You could get at the keys?"

"No." Mickey's tone was emphatic.

"Those who are not with us are against us," Finnegan warned.

"Us?"

"The Young Irelanders."

There! It was out in the open. Somehow Mickey thought O'Brien would be against this. He said as much to Finnegan, who seemed to reflect and back up a bit. "Keep it in mind, kid," he replied lamely, before wandering off.

Mickey watched him go with cold eyes. Men like Finnegan were always dangerous. He continued towards home, and his mother put a bowl of hearty Irish stew in front of him. After eating, he relaxed and spoke with his father about the mining work. He said nothing to his folks about Finnegan. He didn't want to worry them.

Next morning, he found out that a sidekick of Finnegan had made a similar approach to Birdy, and he determined to do something about it. Later, following another hard day in the mines, he spotted O'Brien in the main street of the town and he told the man what his underlings had been up to. The man's face grew stormy as he listened to the lad's tale. "I'll deal with this," he promised the lad. "Don't you worry your head about it anymore."

When Mickey next saw Finnegan, he noticed the man was sporting a few bruises. Finnegan shot him a venomous look but said nothing as he passed him in the street.

O'Brien stopped him later and spoke briefly: "That's sorted."

Mickey nodded his thanks. He put a question of his own.

O'Brien considered the question deeply. "Will we rebel? I think it's inevitable...that's if the church doesn't interfere too much. Bloody priests...they'll destroy this country."

"They're that powerful?"

"You'd better believe it, Mickey. They hold an enormous sway over the people. They undermine my people all of the time...but mark my words...our time is coming!"

"What will you achieve?"

"Irish independence. The right to govern ourselves...a constitutional government up in Dublin."

"High ideals," Mickey commented.

"We have a right to self-determination." The man was dogged in his convictions.

"Didn't Daniel O'Connell set out to achieve that?"

O'Brien frowned. "He went about it in a different way. He didn't espouse doing it by violent ways, and rejected the notion of republicanism. I think history will show him in a good light. He achieved a lot."

"Catholic emancipation?"

O'Brien looked at Mickey in a new light. "You know about that. You're wasting your time in those mines, boy. You've got a grasp of historical matters that would make teachers weep with envy. You're right of course...emancipation removed many of the stumbling blocks faced by Roman Catholics...gave them voting rights...and access to good jobs in the judiciary, military and government. Daniel helped bring about those changes in a big way."

"Do you think Ireland will ever be truly free?"

"Good question," O'Brien commented, his tone reflective. "Some day, the Irish people will say enough is enough, but they'll need to act in concert and get up off their backsides and act. Maybe, then."

There was a short silence. O'Brien's next words contained more than a hint of prophecy. "It could happen when England's backs are turned...when their attentions are preoccupied with more pressing matters on the world stage."

It was a conversation that Mickey was to recall much later in life as he watched his youngest grandson don the uniform of the Citizen army. England was embroiled in a world conflict, and Irishmen and women were about to strike a blow for Irish freedom. At the age of eighty one, his movements slow and ponderous, and crippled with arthritis which he put down to his early mining years, all Mickey could do was watch and pray that his grandson would succeed in a quest that had proved impossible for younger generations, including O'Briens Young Irelanders.

He sighed deeply. "Go with God, my son."

Don't miss out!

Visit the website below and you can sign up to receive emails whenever Liam Robert Mullen publishes a new book. There's no charge and no obligation.

https://books2read.com/r/B-A-HWRD-PUFW

BOOKS 2 READ

Connecting independent readers to independent writers.

About the Publisher

Printed in Great Britain
by Amazon

87819569R00246